GARY ROSENS

CRIME AND PUNISHMENT

THE TECHNIQUES OF
THE OMNISCIENT AUTHOR

LISSE

THE PETER DE RIDDER PRESS

1978

ISBN 90 316 0104 7

Printed in Great Britain
by Western Printing Services, Limited, Bristol

TABLE OF CONTENTS

PREFACE

Is there really a need for another book on Dostoevsky? There has certainly been no lack in the last few decades of articles and books on the structure, ideas, and symbolism of his stories and novels. Yet despite this great wealth of scholarship, and all the attention given the techniques of point of view in German and Anglo-American criticism, few articles and no books have been written on the point of view of Dostoevsky's major fiction.

Many scholars have argued that Dostoevsky, unlike Flaubert and Henry James, was never a conscious craftsman, but a genius who merely used the novel as a vehicle for his ideas. Although critical analysis has done much to disprove such impressionistic notions, no one has systematically demonstrated how Dostoevsky used the techniques of point of view usually associated with modern objectivist fiction and the disciples of Henry James. In fact, Dostoevsky was as interested in narrative technique as was James. Those "loose baggy monsters", as James called the works of Tolstoy and Dostoevsky, were after all being held together by something. Dostoevsky's range, depth, and consuming interest in exploring human psychology led him to experiment with narrators of far greater complexity, if not sophistication, than the American master.

Yet for a long time very little extrinsic evidence existed to demonstrate Dostoevsky's concern with point of view; there were no prefaces, no treatises on the art of the novel, no notebooks written with an eye to future generations. The publication in the 1930's of Dostoevsky's working notebooks for the major novels, however, changed this situation radically. The notebooks provide the evidence which should perhaps have been obvious from the novels themselves. They take us directly into Dostoevsky's creative laboratory and make us eyewitnesses of his internal debates over the best point of view from which to present his work. If, as one critic has noted, *Crime and Punishment* is the story of a murderer in search of the motive for his crime, then the notebooks show that for an even longer time it was a story in search of the appropriate point of view.

I have chosen *Crime and Punishment* to illustrate Dostoevsky's handling of point of view for a number of reasons. The omniscient-author technique makes it easy to compare this novel to other nineteenth- and for that matter twentieth-century novels written in the third person. It displays a greater array of methods for the presentation of consciousness than do any of his other novels. Through the use of an undramatized teller it lends itself to a thoroughgoing analysis of narrative irony, perhaps the most distinguishing characteristic of the eighteenth- and nineteenth-century novel. But most important, it shows clearly and dramatically how Dostoevsky manipulates point of view to achieve stylistic unity and depth of characterization.

For, in the final analysis, point of view in *Crime and Punishment* is not merely a means to an end, it is an essential aspect of the characterization and plot, and the foundation of the evaluative norms by which all the events and personages are judged. Thus an understanding of the purpose of the narrator in *Crime and Punishment* gives us another key for unlocking the mysteries of Raskolnikov's personality and the still imperfectly understood epilogue, by far the most controversial aspect of the novel at the present time.

NOTE ON THE TRANSLITERATION OF RUSSIAN

I have used J. Thomas Shaw's System I for transliterating personal and place names in text and his System III for words as words and all citations of bibliographical material. See Shaw's *The Transliteration of Modern Russian for English-Language Publications* (Madison: Univ. of Wisconsin Press, 1967). System I will help the reader who is not familiar with Russian to pronounce Russian names and places fairly accurately. System III is the international scholarly system for the transliteration of Russian.

Chapter Two is a revised version of "First- versus Third-Person Narration in 'Crime and Punishment,'" *Slavic and East European Journal*, 17 (1973), 399–407. I am grateful to the editor of *SEEJ* for permission to print parts of the article here.

I should like to express my appreciation to J. Thomas Shaw and Victor Terras for their encouragement and many helpful suggestions, especially during the writing of the first several drafts. I should also like to thank James Bailey, Xenia Gasiorowska, Lawrence Thomas, and Elizabeth Uhr for reading the manuscript at various stages of its development and offering their critical comments.

University of Wisconsin
Madison, February 1976

CHAPTER 1

INTRODUCTION

It is not surprising that the narrator's role in *Crime and Punishment* has
received little scholarly attention.[1] Whereas Dostoevsky's other major
novels have personal dramatized narrators, the narrator of *Crime and
Punishment* is comparatively inconspicuous. He is neither the hero, as in
A Raw Youth, nor even a character in his own story as in *The Possessed*
and *The Brothers Karamazov*, and he is a far cry from the garrulous
intrusive author of *The Idiot*. His relative success at escaping detection,
however, has led to unwarranted critical neglect; for of all Dostoevsky's
narrators, he is perhaps the most crucial to our perception of the characters and events. Indeed, it can be argued that the world of *Crime and*

---

[1] Pierre R. Hart's "Looking over Raskol'nikov's Shoulder: The Narrator in
'Crime and Punishment,'" *Criticism*, 13 (1971), 166–79, is to date the most informa-
tive work on the subject. Most of the other work that has been done on the
narration of *Crime and Punishment* is to be found in scattered remarks in various
books and articles. See, for example, Julius Meier-Graefe, *Dostoevsky: The Man
and His Work*, trans. by Herbert H. Marks (New York: Harcourt, 1928), p. 112;
Joseph Warren Beach, *The Twentieth Century Novel: Studies in Technique* (New
York: Appleton, 1932), pp. 155–7, 194–6; F. I. Evnin, "Roman 'Prestuplenie i
nakazanie,'" in *Tvorčestvo Dostoevskogo*, ed. by N. L. Stepanov (M.: AN SSSR,
1959), p. 169; Lászlo Karanči, "K problematike pisatel'noj manery Dostoevskogo," *Slavica*, 1 (1961), 135–55; Ja. O. Zundelovič, *Romany Dostoevskogo:
Stat'i* (Taškent: Srednjaja i vysšaja škola, 1963), pp. 10–61; G. M. Fridlender,
Realizm Dostoevskogo (M. L.: AN SSSR, 1964), pp. 170–4, 190–1; F. I. Evnin,
"O nekotoryx voprosax stilja i poètiki Dostoevskogo," *Izvestija Akademii nauk*,
24, no. 1 (1965), 68–80; Edward Wasiolek, *F. M. Dostoevsky, The Notebooks for
"Crime and Punishment"* (Chicago: Univ. of Chicago Press, 1967), pp. 9–10,
100–2; V. I. Ètov, *Dostoevskij: Očerk tvorčestva* (M.: Prosveščenie, 1968), p. 195;
L. D. Opul'skaja, "Istorija sozdanija romana," in *F. M. Dostoevskij, "Prestuplenie
i nakazanie,"* ed. by L. D. Opul'skaja and F. G. Kogan (M.: Nauka, 1970), p. 688;
A. A. Belkin, *Čitaja Dostoevskogo i Čexova* (M.: Xudožestvennaja lit., 1973),
pp. 73–4; V. N. Toporov, "O strukture romana Dostoevskogo 'Prestuplenie i
nakazanie,'" in *Structure of Texts and Semiotics of Culture*, ed. Jan van der Eng
and Mojmír Grygar (The Hague: Mouton, 1973), pp. 225–302; V. A. Mysljakov,
"Kak rasskazana 'istorija' Rodiona Raskol'nikova," in Dostoevskij: *Materialy i
issledovanija*, ed. G. M. Fridlender (L.: Nauka, 1974), pp. 147–63.

Punishment is the narrator's world. To understand his role in the novel is not only to gain a deeper appreciation of *Crime and Punishment* itself, but to delve into the novel as a literary genre. As Wolfgang Kayser has argued, the lifeblood of the novel is its narrator; without him it is but an empty shell.[2]

Unfortunately, the little that has been done on the narrators of Dostoevsky's other major novels has very limited application to *Crime and Punishment* for two reasons. First, the narrator in *Crime and Punishment* differs greatly from the narrators in Dostoevsky's other works. Dostoevsky rarely used objective third-person narrators, preferring instead a first- or highly dramatized third-person teller. Thus insights, for example, into the first-person mode of *A Raw Youth* can hardly be expected to shed much light on the third-person mode of *Crime and Punishment*. Second, most of the analyses of point of view in Dostoevsky's novels have failed to appreciate the sophistication of his techniques. They have rarely if ever distinguished between the implied author, the narrator, and the historical Dostoevsky, a critical oversight which has led to serious misinterpretations. Few would identify the narrator of *A Raw Youth*, Arkady Dolgoruky, with the implied author or the historical Dostoevsky; but critics have seen Dostoevsky not only in the narrator of *The Possessed*, but also in Makar Devushkin, the hero of *Poor Folk*.[3] Nor is the implied author of Dostoevsky's novels always identical to the historical author. When it is artistically necessary, Dostoevsky presents his most cherished ideas in an ambiguous light. Shatov's ideas on Russian Orthodoxy — virtually identical to Dostoevsky's own — are presented with as much skepticism as Kirillov's ravings on suicide.

The most widespread view on Dostoevsky's narrators is that they are essentially objective, serving a so-called "informational function".[4]

---

[2] See Wolfgang Kayser, *Entstehung und Krise des modernen Romans*, 2nd ed. (Stuttgart: J. B. Metzlersche Verlagsbuchhandlung, 1955).

[3] For an explicit identification of Dostoevsky with Devushkin, see D. S. Lixačev, "Letopisnoe vremja u Dostoevskogo," in his *Poètika drevnerusskoj literatury* (L.: Nauka, 1967), pp. 321–2.

[4] See, for example, A. V. Lunačarskij, "O 'mnogogolosnosti' Dostoevskogo," in *F. M. Dostoevskij v russkoj kritike: Sbornik statej*, ed. A. A. Belkin (M.: GIXL, 1956), p. 413; G. I. Čulkov, *Kak rabotal Dostoevskij* (M.: Sov. pisatel', 1939), pp. 81, 146; Evnin, "*Prestuplenie i nakazanie*," p. 109; L. P. Grossman, "Dostoevskij — xudožnik," in *Tvorčestvo Dostoevskogo*, pp. 353–4; Karanči, p. 142; M. M. Baxtin, *Problemy poètiki Dostoevskogo*, 2nd ed. (M. Sov. pisatel', 1963), p. 336; Fridlender, p. 190; V. I. Ètov, "Manera povestvovanija v romane Dostoevskogo *Idiot*," *Vestnik Moskovskogo universiteta*, 21, No. 1 (1966), 74.

According to this view, Dostoevsky is a dramatic novelist who prefers to show rather than tell, and when he occasionally does narrate, his reports are merely sober concise summaries of the necessary information. In other words, unlike such writers as George Eliot, Dickens, or Gogol, Dostoevsky rarely assumes the role of the intrusive omniscient author. The assertion that Dostoevsky's narrators are objective, however, is a position that cannot withstand critical analysis. If by objectivity we mean little authorial intrusion, then it is true that *Crime and Punishment* is more objective than most of the novels of Dostoevsky's Russian and Western European contemporaries. But it is not nearly so objective as many third-person novels written during the twentieth century, nor so objective as is frequently argued. In fact I intend to demonstrate that the narrator in *Crime and Punishment*, by a variety of means, some subtle and some obvious, plays an essential part in the novel's rhetorical structure.

Even the best analyses of Dostoevsky's narrators are marred by serious analytical flaws. Van der Eng, for example, argues that Dostoevsky uses a different technique for main as against secondary characters.[5] He maintains that whereas Dostoevsky employs traditional omniscience in handling his minor characters, he presents his major characters through speech, action, and the transcription of consciousness, that is, objectively and dramatically. Though van der Eng's confusion of narrator and implied author makes his argument untenable for Dostoevsky's novels as a whole, his description seems at first rather apt for the narrator of *Crime and Punishment*. However, van der Eng's division of characters into two groups is highly debatable. Are Marmeladov, Svidrigaylov, and Porfiry Petrovich really more important than Katerina Ivanovna, Luzhin, and Razumikhin? Furthermore, van der Eng fails to observe that Dostoevsky often uses traditional techniques for his so-called major characters and dramatic techniques for his minor ones.

The most radical approach to the narrator in Dostoevsky's novels was put forward by Mikhail Bakhtin, who, as early as 1929, argued that Dostoevsky's handling of narration marked a revolutionary stage in the development of the novel.[6] Though Bakhtin's generalizations are over-broad and his terminology imprecise, his work is nevertheless provocative. Bakhtin sees the essential difference betwen the Dostoevskian

---

[5] Johannes J. van der Eng, *Dostoevskij romancier: Rapports entre sa vision du monde et ses procédés littéraires* (The Hague: Mouton, 1957), pp. 75–81.

[6] The second edition of Bakhtin's work (see note 4) differs little in its essential argument from the 1929 edition.

(polyphonic) and the traditional (monophonic) novel in the relationship of the dramatis personae to what he calls the author's voice. Whereas in the traditional novel, the author's voice is a dominating structural and evaluating center to which all other voices (points of view) are subordinated; in a polyphonic novel, the author's voice is equal to, but no more important than, the voices of the major characters. Dostoevsky created a new type of novel, according to Bakhtin, by incorporating the point of view of the monophonic narrator into the consciousness of his hero, thereby providing him with the perspective and knowledge of the traditional intrusive author. Since the primacy of the author's voice had to be eliminated if the hero was to become completely independent, Dostoevsky turned his narrator into an objective teller, a mere disseminator of information.

Since Bakhtin rarely distinguishes between the terms "author", "author's voice", and "narrator", it is difficult in many places to understand his exact meaning.[7] Furthermore, the problems created by his imprecise terminology are compounded by his failure to apply his views systematically to Dostoevsky's major fiction. When we use his theories to elucidate point of view in the later novels, we meet with disappointing results. Can the narrator have a point of view equal to that of the characters and yet be merely a disseminator of information? In *The Possessed*, which narrator's point of view is equal to Stavrogin's? The chronicler's? The omniscient author's? Although one might argue that Stavrogin's point of view is as important as the chronicler's, it is certainly not so valid as the omniscient author's. It is true that the point of view of the narrator-hero of *A Raw Youth*, Arkady Dolgoruky, may be no more valid than that of the other characters, but the narrator here is extremely subjective, not at all a mere disseminator of information. In fact, it would seem that Dostoevsky's narrators only reduce the impact of their point of view by openly trying to impose it on others. It is the seemingly objective narrator of *Crime and Punishment*, the narrator who least visibly attempts to subject the characters' points of view to his own, who turns out in the end to be the most successful at doing so. Everything that takes place in *Crime and Punishment* is subordinated to a carefully worked out and decipherable "higher" point of view, and contrary to what Bakhtin maintains, the novel is no more polyphonic than the works of Doestoevsky's contemporaries. Thus the contention that

---

[7] The Russian terms are *avtor* (author), *golos avtora* (author's voice), *rasskazčik* or *povestvovatel'* (narrator).

Dostoevsky increased the objectivity of his narrator in order to ensure the equal validity of all points of view in the novel is erroneous in the case of *Crime and Punishment* and has little if any applicability to Dostoevsky's other major novels.

Actually Dostoevsky's own remarks on the choice of a narrator in *Crime and Punishment* are more enlightening than those of his critics. In a notebook entry dating from a month before the first part of the novel was sent to the publisher, Dostoevsky first entertained the possibility of third-person narration.[8] Until then *Crime and Punishment* had been a first-person confession. In this entry, Dostoevsky proposes an omniscient, infallible, and invisible narrator who would not leave his hero (Raskolnikov) for a moment. In the final version of the novel, the narrator is, indeed, omniscient and infallible; he is not a character in the story, but a superior godlike consciousness who, in accordance with the well-established practice of nineteenth-century fiction, knows everything that takes place both in the external world and in the minds of his characters. The narrator's information and opinions are simply not open to question. They are all substantiated by the plot, symbolism, and structure of the novel. Thus the narrator is, throughout, a spokesman for the implied author.

The narrator of *Crime and Punishment*, however, is not invisible; nor does he stay with Raskolnikov from beginning to end. Dostoevsky must have changed his mind about his original plan some time before he submitted the first part to the publisher, because in the final version of the novel, the narrator is significantly personalized, if not dramatized, and often leaves his hero both to give background material and to transcribe scenes at which Raskolnikov is not present. Unlike the mature James, Dostoevsky makes no attempt to filter all the events through a central intelligence.

---

[8] F. M. Dostoevskij, *Prestuplenie i nakazanie*, ed. L. D. Opul'skaja and G. F. Kogan (Literaturnye pamjatniki; M.: Nauka, 1970), p. 541. Quotations from *Crime and Punishment* and the notebooks for the novel will be directly followed by the page numbers from this edition. References to this edition in the notes will be preceded by *CP*. Unspaced periods will be used to indicate Dostoevsky's ellipses (*points de suspension*); spaced periods indicate my ellipses. All translations from the Russian are mine.

CHAPTER 2

FIRST- VS. THIRD-PERSON NARRATION

The role of the narrator in *Crime and Punishment* evolved slowly and painfully through numerous changes and refinements before it attained its final form.[1] No other aspect of *Crime and Punishment* caused Dostoevsky so many problems. In no other novel did he experience so much difficulty in settling on the right point of view. Only a month before he sent the first part to the publisher, he rejected everything he had written and decided once again to rewrite the entire novel.[2]

Many of the problems that Dostoevsky had with point of view can be ascribed to the novel's unusual evolution. *Crime and Punishment* was actually only one of two works Dostoevsky was writing in the summer of 1865. The other was a projected 330-page novel entitled *The Drunkards*, dealing with the widespread problem of alcoholism in Russian society.[3] This, of course, became the Marmeladov subplot in the final version. At this stage, however, *Crime and Punishment* was planned as a long short story of about sixty pages. The plot was essentially the same as that of the final version. Dostoevsky wrote of it: "The action is contemporary, in the present year. A young man, expelled from the university, petty-bourgeois in origin and living in extreme poverty, as a result of levity and unsound ideas, gives himself to certain strange half-baked notions, which are in the air, and decides at once to break out of his wretched

---

[1] For a detailed account of the evolution of the novel, see L. D. Opul'skaja, "Istorija sozdanija romana," in *CP*, pp. 681-715.

[2] "At the end of November much was written and ready, but I burned everything. I can confess this now. I myself didn't like it. A new form, a new plan carried me away and I began anew." F. M. Dostoevskij, *Pis'ma*, ed. by A. S. Dolinin, I (M., L.: GIXL, 1928), 427.

[3] In a letter to A. K. Kraevsky, the editor of *Notes of the Fatherland* (*Otečestvennye zapiski*), Dostoevsky explains that *The Drunkards* would not only be a general analysis of the question, but a presentation of alcoholism's effect on family life and the upbringing of children. See *Pis'ma*, I, 408.

situation. He has decided to kill an old woman, the wife of a titular councilor, who lends money at interest."[4]

Dostoevsky's financial situation played a major role in transforming the short story into a novel. Harassed by creditors and plagued by ill health, he tried in June 1865 to interest a publisher in *The Drunkards*. Having failed at this, he set aside the novel to work on his story, which he believed was a surer and faster means of procuring funds. However, his efforts to get an advance were in vain. In September, seemingly as a last resort, Dostoevsky offered the story to Katkov's *The Russian Messenger*, a conservative journal in which he had never before published. Katkov accepted Dostoevsky's offer and sent him an advance the following month. Though Dostoevsky promised the work for October, it was far from complete by then; he was already experiencing serious problems with point of view.

A large part of the story in its earliest form has come down to us in Dostoevsky's working notebooks for the novel. This first version is, of course, interesting in itself, but it is particularly valuable because of the light it sheds on the use of the narrator in the final version, especially on Dostoevsky's changing ideas on how best to present Raskolnikov and his crime. What we have of the story is a diary-like confession begun five days after the murder. The extant fragment corresponds to the last part of Part One, and Chapters 1–4 and 6 of Part Two, of the final version. The chapter which included the preparations for the murder and the murder itself is lost. At this stage not a trace is to be seen of the Marmeladov family or of Luzhin and Svidrigaylov.

The only other extant text in the notebooks, written about two months after the story, shows Dostoevsky still using the first-person form even when the narrative has expanded into a novel. This fragment tells us very little about the presentation of Raskolnikov; it is devoted almost entirely to Marmeladov's tavern speech, a scene at which Raskolnikov — as in the final version — is essentially a passive observer.[5]

It is tempting to attribute Dostoevsky's switch from first- to third-person narration to the strain put on the diary by the incorporation of important new characters. After all, if these characters were to be presented strictly from the hero's point of view, Raskolnikov would have to be present at every scene and possess an extraordinary amount of background information. The failure of the hero of *A Raw Youth* to

---

[4] *Iz arxiva F. M. Dostoevskogo: "Prestuplenie i nakazanie,"* ed. I. I. Glivenko (M.: GIXL, 1931), p. 161.

[5] See *CP*, pp. 505–23.

perform a similar but less formidable task gives some indication of the magnitude of the problem. But something even more fundamental than these difficulties lay at the heart of Dostoevsky's decision to change to third-person narration: specifically, the need to dramatize the existential dilemma of his hero.[6]

Fortunately, we possess a passage from the story which in comparison with its counterpart in the final version vividly dramatizes the different effects of the two narrative modes on the presentation of Raskolnikov. It recounts Raskolnikov's escape from the apartment of the murdered pawnbroker. Both passages begin at the point where Raskolnikov has passed the gate of the pawnbroker's house. Although the notebook passages recounting the events immediately preceding this part are missing, subsequent references indicate that the events were similar in both versions. As the passages are quite long, I will break them up and discuss them in sections.

DIARY: How did I have strength for that! My strength was leaving me so quickly that I was beginning to lose consciousness. Recalling now in detail all that happened there, I see that I have almost forgotten not only how I walked along the streets, but even which streets. I remember only that I returned home from

FINAL VERSION: But meanwhile he in no way dared to increase his pace, although about a hundred paces still remained before the first turn. "Shouldn't I slip into some gateway and wait it out on a stairway where I'm not known? No, that would be disastrous! But shouldn't I throw the ax away somewhere? Shouldn't I take a cab? Disaster! Disaster!"

At last the side street. Half dead he turned into it; here he was already half saved and he understood it; less suspicion, besides a crowd was busy milling about and he lost himself in it like a grain of sand. But all these torments had so weakened him that he could

6 Though it is generally assumed that Dostoevsky made a wise choice in switching from first- to third-person narration, no one has discussed this decision in detail. For a representative sample of the literature on the subject, see Julius Meier-Graefe, *Dostoevsky: The Man and His Work*, trans. by Herbert H. Marks (New York: Harcourt, 1928), p. 112; Ralph E. Matlaw, *"The Brothers Karamazov": Novelistic Technique* (Musagetes, 2; The Hague: Mouton, 1957), p. 80; L. P. Grossman, "Dostoevskij — xudožnik," in *Tvorčestvo Dostoevskogo*, ed. N. L. Stepanov (M.: AN SSSR, 1959), p. 389; L. D. Opul'skaja, "Istorija sozdanija romana," in *CP*, p. 688. The most useful remarks on the subject may be found in Edward Wasiolek, ed. and trans., Fyodor Dostoevsky, *The Notebooks for "Crime and Punishment"* (Chicago: Univ. of Chicago Press, 1967), pp. 9–10, 100–2.

the completely opposite direction. I still remember that minute when I got to V. Prospect, but after that I remember little. As in a dream I remember someone's shout near me: "You're really soused!" I was probably very pale or reeling. (431)

hardly move. Sweat poured down in drops; his neck was all wet. "You're really soused!" someone shouted at him as he came out onto the bank of a canal.

He was scarcely conscious of his surroundings now; the further he went, the worse it got. He remembered, however, that suddenly, coming out on the canal, he had taken fright because few people were around and he was more conspicuous, and he almost turned back into the side street. Though he could hardly stand, he nevertheless made a detour and arrived home from an entirely different direction. (70–1)

What is immediately striking about these passages is the degree to which Dostoevsky has altered the focus of attention in the final version. In the diary, although Raskolnikov records his experiences only a week after the murder, he seems separated from his crime by a great physical and psychological distance. We are caught up more with Raskolnikov's mental and physical condition at the time of writing than at the time of the escape. It is as though Dostoevsky were more concerned with the psychology and behavior of the criminal after the crime than before and during it. In every sentence, the narrator imposes himself between the reader and events, emphasizing his present recollection of the past events. In just four sentences, for example, the words "remember" and "recall" are used five times. However, the fact that Raskolnikov remembers things poorly, "as in a dream," makes us feel that the events occurred years and not days before. Raskolnikov considerably strengthens this impression by continually showing surprise at his own actions and by viewing his past self as if it were some alter ego or preposterous double. "How did I have strength for that!" he recalls, marveling at his own physical powers at the time of the murder. "My strength was leaving me so quickly that I was beginning to lose consciousness." Indeed, the narrator's preoccupation with his present memory of the past perhaps indicates that *Crime and Punishment* was originally a psychological study of a criminal only after the murder: for the whole focus, as in *A Raw Youth*, seems to be on the narrator's attempt to assess the meaning of the past for his present situation.

In contrast to the confession, the final version focuses almost exclusively on the time of the events, dramatizing Raskolnikov's physical and emotional ordeal to the greatest possible degree. Every detail involves the reader directly and emotionally. No intervening faulty memories impede the reader's contact with the experiencing Raskolnikov; the reader is, in effect, transported directly into the hero's consciousness as he escapes: "At last the side street. Half dead he turned into it; here he was already half saved and he understood it; less suspicion, besides a crowd was busy milling about and he lost himself in it like a grain of sand." The rhythmic staccato, the telegraphic phrases, the truncated sentences all contribute to the sense of drama and immediacy. The reader is invited to fuse with the hero. That Raskolnikov could lose himself in the crowd like a grain of sand is the wishful thinking of an escaping criminal and not the objective report of an impersonal narrator.

The use of the past tense is another factor significantly enhancing the impact of the final version. In the diary, Raskolnikov's oscillation between past and present, often within the same sentence, repeatedly emphasizes the temporal and psychological distance between his former and present self. The final version, on the other hand, maintains, except for direct quotation, the third-person past tense throughout, thus eliminating the abrupt shift from one temporal plane to another. Since, in contrast to the confession, the past tense is perceived as immediate present, the narrator's descriptions in no way detract from the presentation of Raskolnikov's consciousness during his ordeal. In addition, past tense permits the narrator to shift more smoothly between event, description, and the recording of consciousness, thereby further sharpening the focus on his escaping hero.

Even the paragraph structure reflects the differences between the two versions. In the diary, in which everything is colored by Raskolnikov's imperfect recollection of and emotional response to the murder, the reader follows Raskolnikov's efforts to reconstruct events, rather than the events themselves. The confused impression that Raskolnikov conveys is effective but it dramatizes the present not the past.

The paragraph structure of the final version performs a totally different function. The events are narrated in chronological order, the order in which Raskolnikov experiences, not remembers, them. They are recounted briskly and succinctly; the narrator neither takes part in nor retards the action. At this most suspenseful moment the entire emphasis is on the experiencing, not the remembering Raskolnikov, on the drama of events, not their studied reconstruction.

This emphasis, however, does not detract from the completeness of

Dostoevsky's description. Raskolnikov's thoughts and his very physical condition are constantly set before us. He is shown racked by fear, debilitated, and bathed in perspiration. At every step his mental state is carefully correlated with his physical condition: the internal and external have become one. We can almost feel Raskolnikov jump out of his skin as he hears a passerby calling attention to his prostration: "You're really soused!" when moments before he had thought he had disappeared into the crowd like a grain of sand.

The second paragraph of the final version continues the focus on the experiencing Raskolnikov. Its short paratactic sentences increase the psychological tension and drama of events while swiftly moving the action from the canal to the gate of Raskolnikov's house. Just as in the preceding paragraph, Raskolnikov's physical and mental condition are recorded every step of the way.

At first glance the third paragraph in the final version seems to contain material entirely absent from the diary. But close examination shows it to be not so much an addition to, as a reworking of, the old first-person form. Both versions, for example, note Raskolnikov's dazed condition, his debility, and the fact that he returned home from a completely opposite direction. But even more striking is the unmistakable element of temporal distance in the middle of this paragraph: "He remembered, however, that suddenly, coming out on the canal, he had taken fright because few people were around and he was more conspicuous, and he almost turned back into the side street." Is it possible that the crime is a past event not only for the narrator, but for Raskolnikov as well? One is tempted to say that the word "remembered" is an oversight on Dostoevsky's part. It is known, for example, that Dostoevsky occasionally used the old first-person drafts in writing the final version, in some cases transforming first-person scenes into the third person merely by changing "I" to "he" or "Raskolnikov".[7] Could he have mechanically copied the word "remembered" from the confession? The evidence strongly speaks against such an assumption. There are just too many passages like this one throughout the novel, even discounting those in the epilogue, for it to be a mere slip of the pen. Raskolnikov is continually recollecting

---

[7] This is well illustrated in the variants for Chapter Two, Part One, in which Raskolnikov takes the drunken Marmeladov home and for Chapter Two, Part Two, in which Raskolnikov visits Razumikhin. See *CP*, pp. 520–3, 598–601. It must, however, be mentioned that even with these changes from the first- to the third-person mode, the text of the third-person variants still differs substantially from the final version.

events that occurred to him before, during, and after the murder. The crucial role these passages play in preparing the reader for Raskolnikov's spiritual transformation in the epilogue will be discussed in Chapter Nine.

This reminiscence phrase in the final version, however, produces an entirely different impression from the comparable statements in the diary. In fact, it is so subtly incorporated into the narrative that it almost escapes detection. Since in the third person, past tense is used for the psychological present, the phrase "he remembered", in contrast to the diary, remains relatively inconspicuous. Moreover, it is embedded in a sentence which is so similar in phraseology to what precedes and follows that the reader may simply pass over it. Dostoevsky's method here is by no means accidental. The longer, more analytic reminiscence passages come at clear-cut junctures in the narrative; however, when the focus is on the experiencing Raskolnikov, the passages neither retard the action nor deflate the suspense.

In the next section of text, still another significant difference between the two versions is illustrated: the difference in the narrators.

DIARY: I came to my senses upon entering the gate of our house. No one was there. But I was hardly in a condition any longer to feel fear or take precautions. I was just about to start up the stairs, but suddenly I remembered the ax. It really had to be replaced, it was a matter of the greatest importance, but I even forgot about this, shattered as I was. Oh God, what difficulties there were! Only by a miracle did everything come about in such a way that I passed through all these horrors undetected. (431)

FINAL VERSION: Nor was he fully conscious when he passed through the gateway of his house; at any rate he had already started up the stairs and only then remembered about the ax. But now a very important task stood before him: replacing the ax and doing it as inconspicuously as possible. Of course, he was no longer capable of realizing that perhaps it would be better for him not to put the ax back in its former place at all, but to throw it, even if later on, into someone else's yard. (71)

Though the diary begins with a rather effective description of Raskolnikov's return home and his replacing of the murder weapon, the focus keeps shifting from the experiencing to the narrating self. As in the beginning section from the diary, Raskolnikov interrupts the account of his escape to express his present amazement at his past deeds. "Oh God, what difficulties there were!" The exclamatory phrases, as before, indicate that in the diary Dostoevsky was trying to redirect attention from the experiencing to the narrating self.

The narrator in the final version performs a totally different function. The first two sentences of the section differ little from the previous paragraph: attention is riveted on Raskolnikov making his miraculous escape. The action moves apace; the suspense is at a feverish pitch. But in the third sentence, a curious statement reveals the narrator's own views on Raskolnikov's situation. "Of course, he was no longer capable of realizing that perhaps it would be better for him not to put the ax back in its former place at all, but to throw it, even if later on, into someone else's yard."

Raskolnikov has pretensions of being a sort of moral Napoleon, who can murder successfully and with impunity. He also believes that if he is truly one of the elect he will not experience the eclipse of will that overcomes most criminals during the commission of the crime. Since superior individuals cannot in their own eyes consider their actions in any way criminal, they are not subject to such weaknesses. Raskolnikov's actions, however, show that even in his own terms he is no Napoleon: the successful perpetration of the murder owes less to his physical and mental powers than to chance. Actually he is a bungler and that he murders successfully demonstrates the novel's underlying assumption that human behavior is neither predictable nor rational. The self-proclaimed rationalist loses control of his rational faculties at the most critical moment. It would seem that Raskolnikov's actions alone prove that he has failed the test; yet the narrator personally undercuts Raskolnikov's Napoleonic view of himself by explicitly commenting on his inability to think clearly in time of crisis.

Though critics have seldom noted the narrator's expressed opinions on Raskolnikov, they occur throughout the novel, even, as the above example shows, in the most dramatic passages. Indeed, the presence of an omniscient, morally superior narrator is one of the greatest differences between the diary and the final version. In the diary, the distance separating the remembering and experiencing self, though considerable, is not so much moral as "narrative", that is, it results not from the moral difference between the doer and teller, but from the teller's inability to remember clearly what happened to himself only a week ago. In the final version, narrator and character are separated by not only a temporal, but also an intellectual and moral distance. Throughout the novel, the omniscient author maintains a rigorously critical, though sympathetic, attitude toward Raskolnikov; and, in contrast to the narrator of the diary, he has absolute knowledge not only of past and present but also of the future: from his perspective, even Raskolnikov's conversion represents not a prediction, but an accomplished fact.

Yet, and this is crucial, the narrator's evaluation does not detract from the drama of events any more than did the reminiscence phrase, "he remembered". There is no change of tense for commentary. Furthermore, though it is the narrator who suggests the best way to get rid of the ax, it is conveyed in terms Raskolnikov might himself have used, had he been in full command of his faculties. In addition, the narrator supplies a fact, not a conjecture, to explain Raskolnikov's failure to think clearly. He does not say: "Raskolnikov should have realized that" but "[Raskolnikov] was no longer capable of realizing." Dostoevsky, thus, conveys his narrator's criticism without sacrificing either psychological immediacy or suspense. He has it both ways.

The last sections of the diary and final version, though containing no further surprises, continue to exhibit the same differences in emphasis and point of view.

DIARY: Having descended again toward the gate I saw that the door to the caretaker's room was closed but not locked. So the caretaker was either in or someplace very nearby in the yard. But I had already lost the ability to reason and control myself to such an extent that I approached the door directly, went down the three steps to the caretaker's room, and opened the door wide. What would I have said to the caretaker if he had asked, "What do you want?" I wouldn't have been able to answer at all, and so I would have given myself away by my strange look. But the caretaker

FINAL VERSION: But everything turned out well. The door to the caretaker's room was closed but not locked, so it seemed most likely that the caretaker was in. But he had already lost the ability to reason anything through to such an extent that he approached the caretaker's door directly and opened it. If the caretaker had asked him, "What do you want?" he would perhaps have simply given the ax to him. But the caretaker was again not in, and he managed to

wasn't in. I took out the ax
and put it in its former place
under the little bench, covering it
with a log just as it lay before.
I remember as in a dream
that I was even happy and pleased
when I finished with the ax. Then
I went out, closed the door, and
went to my room. I met no one, not
a solitary soul, right up to my
apartment. The landlady's door was
closed. Once in my room I
immediately threw myself on the bed.
I didn't go to sleep, but fell into a
trance or semi-trance, because if
someone had come into my room at
that time, I would have instantly
jumped up and begun to scream.
Scraps and fragments of thoughts
swarmed in my head in a veritable
whirlwind. But I don't remember
a single one of them. (431–2)

lay the ax in its former
position under the bench;
he even covered it with a
log as before. Afterwards
he met no one, not a solitary
soul, right up to his own
room; the landlady's door
was closed. Once in his
room, he threw himself
on the sofa just as he
was. He didn't sleep, but
lay there in a trance. If
someone had come into his
room then, he would have
instantly jumped up and
begun to scream. Scraps
and fragments of some
vague thoughts were simply
swarming in his head, but
despite his efforts, he
could neither latch on to
nor fix on a single one. ...
(71)

These passages are more alike than the ones already examined. The events follow the same order and the phraseology is often identical. But the emphasis in the diary is still on the narrating, not the experiencing, Raskolnikov: "I *remember as in a dream* that I was even happy and pleased when I finished with the ax. ... Scraps and fragments of thoughts swarmed in my head in a veritable whirlwind. But I don't remember a single one of them." Whereas the wavering between the past and present here dilutes suspense and divides the reader's attention, the final version gains in concentration and momentum by focusing totally on the experiencing Raskolnikov. Dostoevsky effectively minimizes the distance between narrator and the experiencing self so that nothing impedes the reader's course to the breathtaking finale.

The change from first- to third-person narrative, as these quoted sections illustrate, dramatically affects the portrayal of the hero. The inclusion of a unique temporal system enables the narrator to use reminiscence as a means of foreshadowing future events without sacrificing dramatic impact. The new ironic relationship between Raskolnikov and the narrator gives the reader a touchstone for measuring the hero's actions, pronouncements, and thoughts, not after, but as they occur. And the shift in emphasis from a recollecting narrator to the criminal while he is planning, perpetrating, and suffering the consequence of his crime makes the narrative more immediate and vivid and thus involves the reader in the events more directly and emotionally. *Crime and Punishment* becomes a drama not of a remembering, but of an experiencing consciousness.

One of the most obvious advantages of the change in point of view is a marked increase in suspense. Since the murderer is known from the very beginning, the suspense in *Crime and Punishment*, in contrast to that of the standard detective story, is almost totally psychological. We are intrigued not so much by the escape itself as by Raskolnikov's mental, spiritual, and physical condition during the escape. By presenting the events from the experiencing Raskolnikov's point of view, Dostoevsky compels us to share his hero's panic, anxiety, and suffering. Dostoevsky has not abandoned suspense; he transformed it and elevated it to a higher plane.

But most important, an experiencing Raskolnikov is vital to the working out of the novel's main theme: crime and punishment. Raskolnikov's crime does not end or, for that matter, begin with the murder, just as his punishment neither begins nor ends with his deportation to Siberia. If the real crime is atheism and intellectual pride, Raskolnikov is in a state of sin a year before the novel begins and remains so up to his conversion in the epilogue. Similarly, there is no point in the novel where Raskolnikov is not being punished for his crime. Indeed, his condition — physical and psychological — is as bad before the murder as after. Focusing on the experiencing self thus not only makes the murder more vivid and powerful, but dramatizes throughout the novel the psychological, philosophical, and social consequences of the crime and its concurrent punishment. Only by being placed in direct contact with Raskolnikov during the most harrowing moments of his experience, can we fully understand and feel the enormity of his crime and the hell of his punishment.

Moreover, by presenting the events as they occur, third-person narration is able to dramatize much more forcefully than the diary the existential significance of Raskolnikov's suffering. Suffering is, after all, what most engages our sympathy for Raskolnikov and involves us in his fate. It is what he and Sonya have in common, and ultimately it is his means of salvation. But this suffering has to be shown, not described, if we are to appreciate fully the agony of his present situation and what he must endure in order to attain the happiness prophesied for him in the epilogue.

CHAPTER 3

SELECTIVE OMNISCIENCE

Dostoevsky's notebooks demonstrate that the shift from first- to third-person narration in *Crime and Punishment* had much more to do with the presentation of Raskolnikov than the need to deal with a large and varied cast of characters. Yet third-person narration greatly enhanced the portrayal of the major secondary characters, for it provided Dostoevsky with an opportunity to develop them in a manner inconceivable in the framework of a first-person narrative.

Percy Lubbock, in his *Craft of Fiction*, argues that in *Crime and Punishment*, as in James's *The Ambassadors*, the hero's point of view is maintained throughout.[1] *The Ambassadors*, to be sure, is told almost entirely from Strether's point of view: our knowledge of the other characters is confined to what they say in his presence and how they are reflected in his consciousness. The situation in *Crime and Punishment* is quite different, however. Dostoevsky transcribes not only Raskolnikov's point of view, but, in varying degrees, the point of view of many of the major characters, including that of his highly opinionated and personalized narrator.[2]

Dostoevsky develops this selective omniscience gradually. In the first two parts of the novel we see basically with Raskolnikov's eyes. Only one scene, a brief interchange in Part Two between Zosimov and Razumikhin, takes place when Raskolnikov is not present. Starting with Part Three, however, the narrator leaves his hero more and more, transcribing the

---

[1] Percy Lubbock, *The Craft of Fiction* (1921; rpt. New York: Viking, 1957), p. 144. For similar views, see Konstantin Mochulsky, *Dostoevsky: His Life and Work*, trans. by Michael A. Minihan (Princeton: Princeton Univ. Press, 1967), p. 298; L. P. Grossman, "Dostoevskij — xudožnik" in *Tvorčestvo Dostoevskogo*, ed. by N. L. Stepanov (M.: AN SSSR, 1959), p. 389; G. M. Fridlender, *Realizm Dostoevskogo* (M., L.; AN SSSR, 1964), p. 171.

[2] Joseph Warren Beach in *The Twentieth Century Novel: Studies in Technique* (New York: Appleton, 1932), pp. 155–8, 194–7, noted the point of view in *Crime and Punishment* was not restricted to Raskolnikov alone.

consciousness of other characters and including scenes from which Raskolnikov is conspicuously absent. Most of these scenes, varying in length and technique, have to do with the Svidrigaylov-Luzhin subplot. There are, for example, conversations between: Raskolnikov's mother and sister; Razumikhin and Zosimov; Sonya and Luzhin; Luzhin and Lebezyatnikov. We also watch Svidrigaylov follow Sonya to her apartment, and near the end of the novel we witness several of his hair-raising nightmares.

Whereas the requirements of the plot might partially explain the use of different points of view in scenes in which Raskolnikov is absent, they cannot account for the switch to other points of view in scenes in which the hero is present. Yet, not only do we occasionally see through the eyes of other major characters in Raskolnikov's presence, we see through the eyes of minor characters as well. It is evident that Dostoevsky had particular reasons for using a technique of selective omniscience in these passages, reasons that become clear from an examination of the text. I shall therefore discuss several brief passages in which he records the thoughts and feelings of other characters when Raskolnikov is present. The first is from Raskolnikov's meeting with his mother and sister in Chapter Three, Part Three. Razumikhin and Zosimov are also present.

He [Razumikhin] would have seen had he more penetration, that Raskolnikov was in no sentimental mood, in fact, something like the very opposite. But Avdotya Romanovna noticed. She was intently and anxiously observing her brother. (174–5)

In this passage the narrator plainly records the perception of both Dunya and Razumikhin. His report of Dunya's perspicacity, or Razumikhin's lack of it, however, is much more than a mere stage direction; it reveals how Raskolnikov appeared to others at the time and also provides information about Dunya and Razumikhin. The naive, simple-hearted Razumikhin is fooled by Raskolnikov's sentimental facade, not because he is unperceptive, but because he generally takes people at their word, rarely expecting guile. Such passages build up Razumikhin's artlessness, a trait essential to his function as a positive foil to Raskolnikov.

Dunya, however, is not at all fooled by her brother's deception. She sees through his facade just as he has seen through her motives for marrying Luzhin. Brother and sister are very much alike, as Razumikhin later remarks; and here Dostoevsky uses her perception to underscore their spiritual kinship. She, too, knows how to disguise her feelings.

The second passage presents Porfiry Petrovich and Raskolnikov heatedly discussing Raskolnikov's article on crime. Razumikhin is present, but for at least two-thirds of the scene he listens, half in disbelief, closely observing his friends as they engage each other in a battle of intellect and will.

> Raskolnikov raised his pale and almost sorrowful face towards him [Razumikhin] and made no reply. Alongside this quiet and sorrowful face, Porfiry's unconcealed, persistent, provocative, and *discourteous* sarcasm seemed strange to Razumikhin. (205)

Since up to this point the scene has basically been presented through Raskolnikov's eyes, there has been no objective description of how either Porfiry or Raskolnikov looked during the argument. It is true that Porfiry is constantly before us, but his image is distorted by Raskolnikov's jaundiced perception. Is Porfiry scrutinizing Raskolnikov with ironic superiority, openly and contemptuously winking at him, or is this just a figment of Raskolnikov's feverish imagination? And what of Raskolnikov's appearance: Is his mental turmoil becoming physically observable, thus giving Porfiry an additional advantage in drawing him out? How does he look when he is expounding his theory on the superior individual's right to murder in good conscience? By recording Razumikhin's perception directly after Raskolnikov's summary of his article, Dostoevsky provides the necessary objective description: Raskolnikov wears his suffering on his face, and Porfiry's sarcasm and disrespect have perhaps not been Raskolnikov's invention after all.

The last example records the perception of a whole group, the drunken guests at Marmeladov's funeral feast.

> He [Raskolnikov] seemed firm and calm. It became somehow clear to everyone, just by looking at him, that he really knew what it was all about, and that the solution was at hand. (310)

Raskolnikov has just interceded for Sonya, who has been falsely accused by Luzhin of having stolen one of his banknotes. Up to this point, the center of attention has been Katerina Ivanovna, whom we observe alternately through the eyes of Raskolnikov and the narrator. The crowd has sided with Luzhin against Sonya, but it is beginning to waver after hearing Lebezyatnikov's accusations. Raskolnikov's speech turns the crowd completely against Luzhin. It is nevertheless strange that the guests should give more credence to the word of a haggard and wretchedly dressed student than to the fashionably turned out and pompously proper Mr. Luzhin. Dostoevsky explains their behavior by briefly recording their perception of Raskolnikov as he begins his speech: his look convinces everyone that he is telling the truth. The switch in point of view here is only two sentences long, but it is enough to motivate psychologically what otherwise might have been a rather improbable denouement.

Thus, although Dostoevsky generally confines the point of view to Raskolnikov (and the narrator), he does not hesitate to transcribe the consciousness of secondary and minor characters in Raskolnikov's presence, whenever it is artistically necessary. Though this may seem arbitrary or unsystematic to those schooled in the precepts of Jamesian criticism, it was a common enough nineteenth-century practice, and in *Crime and Punishment* it enhances far more than it detracts from the narrative.[3]

These switches in point of view are invariably brief, however, for Dostoevsky does not wish to retard the flow of events or displace Raskolnikov as the focus of attention when he is present. It is in those scenes from which Raskolnikov is absent that the narrator manifests the full extent of his omniscience by delving into the inner lives of various characters at great length.

He is indeed selective. He exposes the consciousness of Luzhin, Svidrigaylov, and Razumikhin, but rarely reveals the inner emotional and mental lives of Dunya, Pulkheria Alexandrovna, Marmeladov, Katerina Ivanovna, Sonya, and Porfiry Petrovich. Dostoevsky's choice, however, is never arbitrary. In every instance, it leads to a more convincing presentation of the character, and ultimately to a deeper understanding of the problems of his hero.

Porfiry Petrovich, for example, is presented almost totally from Raskolnikov's point of view. Raskolnikov is present not only when Porfiry appears in person, but at all times Porfiry is spoken about by third parties. By presenting him in this manner, Dostoevsky establishes his enigmatic position in the novel, both for Raskolnikov and the reader, thereby heightening psychological suspense. This technique of denying an inner view in order to add mystery is one that Dostoevsky frequently resorted to: it is employed in the characterization of Versilov in *A Raw*

---

[3] For additional examples of the point of view of other characters in scenes at which Raskolnikov is present, see *CP*, pp. 154, 175, 176, 179, 229, 237, 239, 243, 244, 292–4, 297, 299, 312–13, 316, 318, 319, 322, 343, 398.

Youth and Stavrogin in *The Possessed*, but nowhere is it used with more effectiveness than in the presentation of Porfiry.

An examination of the other five major characters for whom there is no inner view makes it apparent that Dostoevsky does not withhold an inner view solely to create mystery: Sonya Marmeladov, Katerina Ivanovna, and Pulkheria Alexandrovna are after all hardly mysterious characters. An inner view of Marmeladov is unnecessary because he turns his soul inside out to anyone who will listen.[4] Although his words do not explicitly reveal his whole personality, they provide enough information to enable the reader to deduce the cause of his many failures. The same is true for Katerina Ivanovna. There seems to be nothing in her conscious life that she will not divulge to others. What she says and does, as well as what Sonya and Marmeladov say about her, reveal enough about Katerina Ivanovna's social pride and deteriorating physical and mental condition to make an inner view superfluous.

Though Raskolnikov's mother and sister are treated from the outside, they are presented quite differently from the Marmeladovs. Having maintained their courage and dignity, they cannot really be expected to open up their souls so freely. Yet Dostoevsky finds a way to disclose their thoughts and feelings: Pulkheria Alexandrovna writes a detailed letter to her son in which so much is revealed about Dunya and herself that an inner view becomes unnecessary.[5]

Sonya Marmeladov is perhaps the only character for whom an inner view would have been not only superfluous, but even detrimental. Sonya's simplicity and frankness of course make the detailed transcription of her consciousness unnecessary; deception is simply alien to her character. Sonya functions not as an independent personage in her own right, but as an antithesis to Raskolnikov; not as a full-bodied woman, but as a symbol of intuitive wisdom and boundless faith. She is more the stuff of allegory than of psychological fiction, and this is the way Dostoevsky intended her. In the notebooks, as soon as he saw Sonya as the vehicle for Raskolnikov's resurrection, he began to make her less and less psychologically ambiguous and complex. She could not remain a woman torn by inner contradictions and still function as the allegorical

---

[4] From the early notebook plans, Marmeladov was conceived as telling his own story. See *CP*, 491–7, 506–24.

[5] There is one notable exception, a long passage in which the narrator reveals Pulkheria Alexandrovna's consciousness through interior monologue. See the discussion of this passage on pp. 42–4.

representative of divine wisdom, and thus the means to Raskolnikov's salvation.

Whereas Dostoevsky's ingenious use of action, letters, and dialogue is, with minor exceptions, perfectly adequate for portraying most of Raskolnikov's foils; Luzhin and Svidrigaylov require a more extensive inner view. Raskolnikov's point of view in this regard is clearly inadequate: Raskolnikov hates both Luzhin and Svidrigaylov and can hardly be trusted to be objective. Neither could they be presented, as Marmeladov and Katerina Ivanovna are, solely through their words and deeds. They are clearly too secretive and devious for that. Yet the presentation of Svidrigaylov's and Luzhin's consciousness is as important to our understanding of Raskolnikov as are the confessions of the Marmeladovs. Therefore an inner view becomes indispensable. It is the only way their thoughts, feelings, and motivations can be exposed.

Raskolnikov's intense dislike of Luzhin, for example, differs significantly from the narrator's. Luzhin's mean-mindedness and thirst for power do not bother Raskolnikov half as much as his status as Dunya's fiancé, since as such Luzhin epitomizes the great sacrifice that Raskolnikov's sister and mother are making for his sake. Raskolnikov's hostility toward Luzhin then results as much from pride as it does from love of family. Furthermore, Raskolnikov's recognition that his own ideas have been taken to their logical conclusion by Luzhin intensifies his hatred not only for his sister's fiancé, but for himself as well. At their first meeting Raskolnikov screams at Luzhin: "Take what you've just been preaching to its logical conclusions and it becomes permitted to slit people's throats." (119) Raskolnikov knows of what he speaks.

Luzhin's actions, however, do not reveal the full extent of his baseness. It is true that he shows himself to be a disagreeably pompous, prim, and self-righteous cad in his relationship with his betrothed and her mother; but not until Dostoevsky exposes his motives can the nature and extent of his evil be properly understood. Only then does Luzhin, like Svidrigaylov, emerge as a living caricature of Raskolnikov's most predatory drives and pernicious theories. No less than Raskolnikov, Luzhin is infected with a desire to wield power over others. Raskolnikov tells Sonya in Part Four that the solution to their respective problems lies in smashing everything and assuming power: "Freedom and power, but above all power! Over all trembling creation, over the whole antheap! ..." (255) Luzhin's desire to exert power is manifested most clearly in his relationship with Dunya. Dostoevsky employs an inner view to dramatize the parallel with Raskolnikov: "She was even more than he had dreamed of; here was a proud and virtuous girl of character, superior to him in education and breeding (he felt this) and such a creature would be slavishly grateful to him her whole life for his noble deed and with reverence abase herself before him and he would have boundless power over her! ..." (239)

Dostoevsky also uses an inner view to underline the similarity between Raskolnikov's and Luzhin's pride and confidence in their innate superiority. Raskolnikov seems convinced that he is intellectually superior to others, that like Napoleon he is destined "to say a new word". The novel, however, shows that he possesses neither the intuitive wisdom of Sonya, the practical common sense of Razumikhin, nor the psychological insight of Porfiry Petrovich. Raskolnikov recognizes in his more lucid moments that he is more a parody than the equal of Napoleon, but these glimpses of the truth are not enough to humble his intellectual pride: only the cleansing fires of suffering accomplish that.

Luzhin's feeling of superiority manifests itself in petty vanity and the contemplation of his own nobility. Since these feelings are exposed less in Luzhin's actions than when he is alone, Dostoevsky is compelled to resort to an inner view. In the following passage, the narrator takes the opportunity to comment on Luzhin's character.

> This conviction was considerably strengthened by vanity and that degree of self-assuredness which may best be called self-infatuation. Peter Petrovich, having made his way up from nothing, had become almost morbidly infatuated with himself, thought highly of his intelligence and abilities and sometimes, when alone, even admired himself in the mirror. ... Yet, he still thought highly of his decision to raise Dunya to his level and considered it a noble deed. Mentioning it to Dunya, he expressed this secret, cherished thought, which he himself had so often admired, and could not understand how others could not admire it too. When he had come to visit Raskolnikov, he entered with the feeling of a benefactor, prepared to reap his rewards and hear very flattering compliments. But now, of course, as he descended the stairs, he considered himself extremely offended and unappreciated. (237–8)

This passage is shot through with irony and sarcasm. Selective omniscience is useful not only in exposing the thoughts of the secretive Luzhin, but also in subjecting them to the critical evaluation of the narrator.

The inner view also underscores the differences between Luzhin and Raskolnikov, for example, their completely different attitudes toward money. Raskolnikov is little concerned with money and when he does consider it, he views it only as a means to an end: to help his mother and sister; to further his career; to devote himself to humanity. Although robbery is the ostensible goal of the murder, Raskolnikov buries the pawnbroker's purse without even looking to see if there is any money in it. Furthermore, his sole positive actions in the novel proper involve the giving of money to people in distress: twice to Katerina Ivanovna and once to a policeman to help a young girl who has just been seduced.

Luzhin, on the other hand, is lowered in our eyes (and Raskolnikov consequently raised by contrast) by his worship of material gain. "But more than anything else in the world, he loved and valued his money, gotten by hard work and various other means." (237) "He was staying with him [Lebezyatnikov] on his arrival in Petersburg not totally out of niggardly economy, although this, in fact, was almost the main reason." (281) It is true that we learn something of Luzhin's miserliness and devotion to business above all else from Pulkheria Alexandrovna's letter to Raskolnikov, but this is a secondhand report: one may, after all, question Pulkheria Alexandrovna's truthfulness and naiveté. Only by delving into Luzhin's inner life can Dostoevsky reveal Luzhin's complete reduction of human relationships to profit. The technique Dostoevsky uses most effectively for accomplishing this task is interior monologue. In the following passage the narrator captures Luzhin still smarting over his recent setback at the Raskolnikovs'.

"It was another mistake not to give them any money at all," he thought, dolefully returning to Lebezyatnikov's room, "and why the hell was I such a Jew? And calculation didn't even enter into it! I thought I'd keep them as badly off as possible so that they would view me as their Providence, and now they go! ... Damn it! ... Had I spent some fifteen hundred rubles for the dowry, for example, for gifts, fancy little boxes, dressing cases, jewelry, fabric, and all that rubbish from Knopp's and the English store, then my proposition would have been better and ... stronger. It wouldn't have been so easy to refuse me now. They are the sort of people who would have certainly considered it their duty to return both the presents and the money in the event of a refusal; and to return all that would have been difficult and painful. And besides, their consciences would not have been at peace: 'How can we suddenly drive away a man who up to now has been so generous and so tactful? ... Hm!' I really made a blunder." (280)

Luzhin can think only in terms of money. His world is so circumscribed by pecuniary dealings that he cannot conceive that others might be

motivated by anything else. He even thinks that he can buy Dunya's conscience for fifteen hundred rubles worth of trinkets. Given the narrator's
esteem for Dunya, such a thought serves to further blacken Luzhin's
character. The passage also provides the motivation for the very next
scene, in which Luzhin attempts to defame Sonya by falsely accusing her
of stealing one of his banknotes. Luzhin is consistent throughout: his
actions are but the extension of his consciousness. He, like Raskolnikov,
is a criminal; only his weapon is different: Raskolnikov wields an ax;
Luzhin a banknote.

The inner view is also essential to the presentation of Svidrigaylov.
Svidrigaylov obviously could not be objectively presented through
Raskolnikov's biased perception and he is too secretive to be presented
solely through his own words. It is true that he is rather garrulous, but
he reveals only what serves his own interest. Even his actions do not
adequately represent his true nature. His gifts to his fiancée, for example,
certainly cannot be interpreted as disinterested generosity or awakened
remorse. Furthermore, the novel is never perfectly explicit about what
Svidrigaylov has done and what he is only reputed to have done. We
never really know whether or not he has three murders on his conscience.
Thus, toward the end of the novel, Dostoevsky utilizes the inner view in
order to dispel the enigma of Svidrigaylov's deeds and to expose his
spiritual bankruptcy and profound despair.

Dostoevsky achieves this end by presenting Svidrigaylov's consciousness totally through nightmares, which effectively transform him, without
a word of commentary by the narrator, into the stuff of his terrible and
repulsive hallucinations. They show the inevitable consequences of self-
interested amoralism and willful isolation from the community of men.
Svidrigaylov is no superman; he is driven to suicide (in Dostoevsky's
world the most cowardly and reprehensible of all deaths) by his inability
to bear the horrors of his dreams. Dostoevsky's inner view, therefore, not
only destroys the enigma of Svidrigaylov, it also dramatizes vividly and
concretely the path that lies before Raskolnikov if he chooses to follow
in Svidrigaylov's footsteps. Only by laying consciousness against consciousness, could Dostoevsky make the parallels between Svidrigaylov
and Raskolnikov apparent and objectively verifiable. For this the inner
view was absolutely essential.

But just as with Luzhin, the inner view is necessary to emphasize not
only the similarities between Svidrigaylov and Raskolnikov but also the
differences. Particularly striking is the difference between Svidrigaylov's
nightmares on the night of his suicide and Raskolnikov's dream of an old

mare savagely beaten to death by a group of drunken peasants. Svidrigaylov's nightmares are without exception revolting and dispiriting.
Moreover, they become progressively worse as the night wears on, ultimately bringing him to a point where suicide becomes the only way to
achieve peace. Raskolnikov's dream, however, terrible as it is, is really
a beneficent one. Its direct consequence is to steer Raskolnikov temporarily away from the contemplated murder of the pawnbroker, and his
own symbolic suicide: "He stood up, looked around in amazement, as
though surprised that he had come here, and went towards T—v Bridge.
He was pale, his eyes burned, and fatigue had leadened his limbs, but he
suddenly began to breathe more easily. He felt that he had thrown off the
terrible burden that had weighed upon him for so long, and suddenly
experienced a sense of relief and peace. 'Lord,' he prayed, 'show me
the way, I renounce that accursed ... dream of mine.' " (51) In addition
to pointing to the suppressed religious side of Raskolnikov's personality,
the dream dramatizes more than anywhere else in the novel the spontaneous, generous, and sympathetic impulses of Raskolnikov's heart (his
empathy for and attempt to help the suffering horse, also a symbol of
the suffering Christ), and thus reveals his potential for spiritual regeneration through suffering.

The only other character for whom Dostoevsky employs an extensive
inner view is Razumikhin. Though his consciousness is exposed in just
two passages, they are long enough to merit close attention. Razumikhin
is, of course, presented as the practicable alternative to Raskolnikov, and
Dostoevsky seems to do everything in his power to underscore his role as
a contrasting character foil. Razumikhin's material situation differs from
Raskolnikov's only in that it is worse. But undaunted by hardships, he
shows that it is possible to overcome poverty and make one's way in the
world without destroying one's fellowman. He is thus a corrective not
only to Raskolnikov, but to Luzhin, Svidrigaylov, and even to the
Marmeladovs. Although Razumikhin's actions indicate what manner of
man he is, and the narrator tells us explicitly about all his virtues long
before he makes his first appearance, Dostoevsky resorts to an inner
view to present Razumikhin's thoughts. If Razumikhin is to be a realistic
and attractive alternative to Raskolnikov, he cannot be presented totally
by explicit praise and virtuous action: at some point, he, like Luzhin and
Svidrigaylov, has to be shown from within. Unlike Sonya, he functions
not as a symbol, but as a psychological type with deep roots in everyday
reality. If Sonya symbolizes the goal for which Raskolnikov must strive,
Razumikhin demonstrates a commendable way to its attainment.

In the following passage, Dostoevsky uses the inner view to compare Razumikhin as favorably as possible with Luzhin. Razumikhin here recalls his improper behavior on the previous night before Dunya and her mother.

His most horrifying recollection was that he had shown himself "vile and base" yesterday, not only because he was drunk, but because out of stupid impulsive jealousy he took advantage of the young girl's situation and rebuked her fiancé to her face, knowing little of their mutual relationship and obligations and hardly anything about the man himself. And just what right did he have to judge him so hastily and rashly? Just who had appointed him judge? Could it be that such a being as Avdotya Romanovna would give herself to an unworthy man for money? That means there must be some worth to the man. The hotel rooms? But could he really tell what the rooms would be like? And after all he was getting an apartment ready. ... Phew, how vile all this was! And what kind of justification was it that he was drunk? It was a stupid excuse, which was even more humiliating for him! ... What was he in comparison to such a girl, — he, yesterday's drunken ruffian and braggart? "Is such a cynical and ridiculous comparison even possible?" (163–4)

Razumikhin's naiveté, ebullience, and charm are as evident in his thoughts as in his actions. He chides himself for behaving so crassly, in particular for abusing Luzhin to Dunya's face: he had no right to judge; and how could he even think that a girl like Dunya would choose a man of little worth. He sees himself as nothing in comparison with her; he literally worships her. The night before he had told her: "I am not worthy to love you, but to worship you is every man's obligation unless he is no more than a brute beast." (158) Whereupon he threw himself down on the pavement and asked to kiss her hands. Razumikhin is ashamed to have taken advantage of Dunya's situation, though he was intoxicated and not in complete control of himself. He questions his motives and belittles his own worth in comparison to hers. In contrast to Razumikhin, Luzhin coldly and calculatingly plans to use Dunya to further his own interests, lauds his motives, and gloats over the prospect of subjecting her to his will. His fondest dream is to have Dunya worship him and him alone: "In deepest secret he had ecstatic visions of a girl, virtuous and poor (she had to be poor), very young, very pretty, well-born and well-educated, very timid, one who had experienced a great deal of misfortune and who would completely humble herself before him, a girl who would her whole life consider him her salvation, would worship him, be subservient to him, admire him, and him alone." (238) Luzhin must be, to use Razumikhin's words, "no more than a brute beast".

The inner view of Razumikhin also contains a strongly implied criticism of Svidrigaylov's relationship with Dunya. Though Svidrigaylov, like Razumikhin, worships Dunya, his worship is based almost totally on sensuality and thus represents as great a perversion of love as does Luzhin's desire for domination.

Razumikhin's relationship with Dunya represents a practical ideal. Whereas Svidrigaylov and Luzhin are presented as exploiters, who view Dunya as an object to be used to further their own interests, Razumikhin is cast in the role of the medieval knight, pleading to be but the servant of his lady. Whereas Luzhin's and Svidrigaylov's sexuality expresses itself in lust and domination, Razumikhin achieves a healthy confluence of the physical and the ideal. Razumikhin's relationship with Dunya thus also serves as an effective contrast to Raskolnikov's relationship with Sonya. In the novel proper, and even through most of the epilogue, Raskolnikov treats Sonya rather harshly, tormenting as often as helping her. Furthermore, he and Sonya are essentially sexless. Though, in the novel, the lack of any sexual involvement between Raskolnikov and Sonya is necessary to the growth of their mutual respect and love, it is implied that this is only a temporary stage and that a more complete relationship, similar to the one worked out for Razumikhin and Dunya, awaits them in the future. Thus in addition to obviating the imbalance that would have occurred had only Raskolnikov's negative foils been presented from within, the inner view of Razumikhin provides an effective means for comparing and evaluating the novel's most important male–female relationships.

CHAPTER 4

INTERIOR MONOLOGUE

The transcription of conciousness plays a greater role in *Crime and Punishment* than it does in any of Dostoevsky's other novels. The consciousness of Raskolnikov is directly, repeatedly, and extensively explored. Since in *The Possessed* and *The Brothers Karamazov* the focus of attention is divided among several figures of nearly equal importance and the story itself is largely told from the point of view of one of the minor characters, the consciousness of the protagonists is seldom presented in detail. We get no inner view of Peter Stepanovich or Stavrogin in *The Possessed*, and even in *The Brothers Karamazov*, where hallucinations, dreams, and interpolated poems are used to give insight into the psyches of the three brothers, much of the characterization is worked out in chapter-long dialogues. In *Crime and Punishment*, however, Raskolnikov occupies center stage throughout most of the novel. Furthermore, partly as a result of the use of third-person omniscience, the novel gives a detailed presentation of the mental and spiritual life not only of Raskolnikov, but of several other important characters. Whereas the last two chapters addressed themselves to the reasons for Dostoevsky's use of a third-person narrator to present an inner view of the characters, this chapter and the next examine the methods he employed.

In *Crime and Punishment*, Dostoevsky uses three techniques of transcribing consciousness: interior monologue, interior analysis, and narrated consciousness. In each technique, the narrator plays a crucial role; for it is usually he who functions as the medium through which the mental and emotional life of the characters is translated into literary language; he must structure and verbalize the frequently amorphous and largely preverbal material of consciousness. In fact, in a third-person narrative, even conversation is a mediated process. Although we may assume that in transcribing conversation the narrator is giving back exactly what was said, the very fact that he is giving us a written and not a spoken record indicates that we have a representation — no doubt a very accurate one, but a representation nevertheless. The fact that even dialogue is a mediated process clearly reveals the great amount of mediation involved in reporting consciousness.

Though the means of transcribing consciousness are all mediated, they differ greatly in form and function. The least mediated of the techniques for transcribing consciousness is interior monologue. Although not all critics define interior monologue in the same way — and some insist the only true interior monologue ever written is to be found in Joyce — it is safe to say that interior monologue occurs in novels written in the third person and that it employs the first-person present tense to transcribe the immediate present for the characters.[1] In other words, it uses the tense and person of direct discourse, and consequently will almost always contrast with the surrounding narrative, which is in the third-person past tense.

Much of the effectiveness of interior monologue in dramatizing thoughts and feelings can be ascribed to this contrast. In a third-person novel in which the narrative tense is primarily past, the shift into interior monologue gives us the feeling of greater psychological immediacy and depth. Although it is the narrator who is actually verbalizing and structuring the amorphousness of consciousness, his personal presence is negligible. He neither ironizes nor comments on what is going on; he merely transforms and transcribes; everything is told strictly from the characters' point of view. Thus a greater degree of personalization comes with the use of first person, for each character's consciousness almost

----

[1] Interior monologue and stream of consciousness are terms often confused, even by those who insist they are totally different. The problem, it seems to me, is tied up with the more experimental psychological fiction of the twentieth century, in which novelists have attempted to represent the ebb and flow of consciousness at preverbal levels. Stream of consciousness is supposed to designate only the subject matter (the mind in flux), whereas interior monologue is the technique by which the flux is transformed into literary language; but the two are so often found together that in practice it is almost impossible to separate them. Moreover, interior monologue may be a misnomer when used to describe the transcription of consciousness at preverbal levels; for, after all, the term implies speech, and before the twentieth century the technique was reserved for recording a sort of internal debate within a character, arising out of a conflict between duty and desire. For the standard statements on the subject, see Lawrence E. Bowling, "What is Stream of Consciousness Technique?" *PMLA*, 65 (1950), 333–45; Robert Humphrey, *Stream of Consciousness in the Modern Novel* (Berkeley: Univ. of California Press, 1954); Melvin Friedman, *Stream of Consciousness: A Study in Literary Method* (New Haven: Yale Univ. Press, 1955); Robert Scholes and Robert Kellogg, *The Nature of Narrative* (London: Oxford Univ. Press, 1966), pp. 177–206; Dorrit Cohn, "Narrated Monologue: Definition of a Fictional Style," *Comparative Literature*, 18 (1966), 97–112.

always bears the impress of his idiosyncrasies of speech and thought. He seems to be presenting himself rather than being presented by someone else. The difference in tense and person of interior monologue from the surrounding narrative does not detract from this psychological immediacy. Since the narrative past is regularly used to indicate the immediate present, interior monologue does not introduce a temporal rift, but rather takes us into a deeper level of consciousness.

Interior monologue is, in most cases, also quite sustained: the narrator rarely breaks into the flow of consciousness to insert his point of view or proceed with the action. This permits the reader to eavesdrop on the character for a considerable time, and, in the process, become more involved in his thoughts and feelings.

Although interior monologue began to be employed extensively and systematically only in the twentieth century, it has a distant relative in classical literature, where it existed in the form of a more or less declamatory oration, delivered in the presence of a confidant. Generally, it conformed rather strictly to the laws of classical rhetoric, being aimed not so much at recording the flow and giving the feel of consciousness as at reproducing the logic of the character's position. Dido's speech to her old nurse before immolating herself is a notable example. So, of course, are most of the great soliloquies in Shakespeare. Hamlet's famous "To be or not to be", with its long periods, carefully constructed parallelisms, and hypothetical questions shows all the earmarks of the classical monologue.

> Who would fardels bear,
> To grunt and sweat under a weary life,
> But that the dread of something after death,
> The undiscovered country from whose bourn
> No traveller returns, puzzles the will,
> And makes us rather bear those ills we have
> Than fly to others that we know not of? (III.i.76–82)

In modern psychological fiction, and especially in the works of Joyce and Virginia Woolf, the monologue turns inward in order to give a more accurate verbal representation of the feel and flux of consciousness, paradoxically at pre- or nonverbal levels. It substitutes impression, associative logic, and the appearance of disorder for the rigid structure, conscious reasoning, and sophisticated expression of the old monologue.[2]

---

[2] For a detailed discussion of the nature and development of interior monologue from Homer to Joyce, see Scholes and Kellogg, pp. 177–206.

Interior monologue is often assumed to be a twentieth-century inno-
vation; but as far back as 1857, the Russian radical critic Nikolay
Chernyshevsky noted the technique in the short stories of Tolstoy.[3]
Dostoevsky also used it, but not nearly so often or in so extreme a form
as James Joyce or Virginia Woolf. From a historical perspective, then,
Dostoevsky seems to represent a midpoint in the development and transformation of the monologue as a literary device. In the interior mono-
logues of *Crime and Punishment*, he attempts to reproduce the emotional
aspects of consciousness in a clearly rhetorical framework, thus combin-
ing the argument of the classical monologue with the feel of consciousness that is the characteristic of its modern counterpart. Yet in *Crime
and Punishment*, the specific nature of interior monologue is invariably
determined by context: sometimes Dostoevsky is more interested in the
emotional turmoil of consciousness, at other times, in its logical movement.

Several passages in Dostoevsky's work indicate that he was acutely
aware of the problems of transcribing consciousness. In them he takes
the reader into his confidence and airs his own views on reproducing the
inchoate thoughts and emotions of his characters. They are important
enough for an understanding of Dostoevsky's method to be quoted in
full.

> That is the theme [of the story]. Of course, the telling of the story takes
> several hours, what with its fits and starts, changes back and forth, and
> confusing form. Now he [the narrator] converses with himself, now it
> is as though he were addressing an invisible listener, some type of
> judge. And that is how it always is in reality. If a stenographer could
> have eavesdropped on him and taken down everything, then it would
> have come out somewhat less smooth and polished than I have pre-
> sented it, but it seems to me the psychological order would perhaps
> have remained the same. ("A Gentle Spirit")[4]

> He recalled it and grew more and more reflective. It is well known that
> entire trains of thought sometimes pass through in our brains instan-
> taneously in the form of certain sensations without being translated
> into human language, not to speak of literary language. But we will
> try to translate all these sensations of our hero and present to the

[3] N. G. Černyševskij, *Literaturno-kritičeskie stat'i*, ed. N. F. Bel'čikov (M.:
GIXL, 1939), pp. 245–57. Chernyshevsky not only described the technique in detail,
but also used the term "interior monologue" (*vnutrennij monolog*) (p. 249).

[4] From the preface to "A Gentle Spirit" (*Krotkaja*), in F. M. Dostoevskij,
Sobranie sočinenij (M.: GIXL, 1956–8), X, 379.

reader at least the essence of these sensations, so to speak, what is most essential and probable in them. For many of our sensations, when translated into ordinary language, appear absolutely improbable. That is why they never even become conscious, whereas everyone has them. ("An Unpleasant Predicament")[5]

Even though "A Gentle Spirit" is a first-person monologue, in it Dostoevsky was confronted with the same problems in presenting consciousness as he was in *Crime and Punishment*. His note in the preface probably was written to prepare the reader for a literary device that at that time might have been confusing and annoying. The unusual form of the story reflects Dostoevsky's attempt to record the actual feel and movement of consciousness.

In the passage from "An Unpleasant Predicament", a work written several years before *Crime and Punishment*, Dostoevsky is somewhat more specific about the relation between consciousness and the methods of recording it. The narrator must try to translate the sensations of thought into literary language, because the reader will give little credence to a verbal representation of raw consciousness, especially when such sensations remain, for the most past, at a subliminal level in the psyche.

Dostoevsky was therefore intent on presenting the feel of consciousness as well as its content and logic. And in practice, he tried to combine the two, rendering the feel of consciousness within the rhetorical framework and conventions of the classical monologue. Each section of interior monologue has its own carefully constructed balance between these two essential characteristics.

Pulkheria Alexandrovna's anxiety at her first meeting with her son is an example in which the feel or flux of consciousness receives particular emphasis. This is an especially important passage because it represents the only inner view of Pulkheria Alexandrovna in the novel.

"And how well he does everything," his mother thought to herself. "What noble impulses he has, and how simply and delicately he put an end to yesterday's misunderstanding with his sister, and all he did was extend his hand at the right moment with a kind look. ... And what beautiful eyes he has, how handsome he is! ... He is even better looking than Dunechka. ... But, my God, what a frightful suit he has on; how terribly dressed he is! Vasya the errand boy in Afanasy Ivanovich's shop is better dressed! ... Oh if only, if only I could rush to him and

---

[5] From "An Unpleasant Predicament" (*Skvernyj anekdot*), in *Sob. soč*, IV, 15–16.

embrace him and ... weep, but I'm afraid, so afraid ... oh, Lord, how strange he is! ... Well, he does speak affectionately, but I'm still afraid! But what am I afraid of? ... " (175)

Pulkheria has not seen Raskolnikov since he left for school several years ago, and though she is overjoyed to be with her son, she is understandably upset by his physical condition and his open hostility to Dunya and herself. When Raskolnikov finally begins to show some joy at seeing his family, Dostoevsky lets his readers personally experience Pulkheria Alexandrovna's initial exultation along with her more deep-seated anxieties.

The monologue is divided into two sections of equal length. In the first half, Pulkheria Alexandrovna is carried away, exulting in Raskolnikov's new warmness and his striking good looks. By the middle of the paragraph, however, her joy becomes clouded by a more objective appraisal of Raskolnikov's appearance, which is, in fact, deplorable, and his warmth, which is largely affected. The paragraph clearly emphasizes the emotional element of consciousness. It is saturated with question marks, exclamations, particles, and sentence fragments. The ellipses, indicating breaks in thought, occur eight times in but a dozen sentences. At the end of the paragraph, where Pulkheria Alexandrovna's fears begin to emerge and she seems to be losing control of herself, the syntax breaks down almost entirely; each thought is expressed in only a word or two: the very sentence structure, as it were, parallels and reflects her mood.

Though one can argue that Pulkheria Alexandrovna's thoughts and emotions are typically maternal (and undoubtedly they were so designed), they are nevertheless considerably individualized, so that she emerges as a real human being, whose suffering is comparable to her son's. Her boundless admiration for her son, of course, lies at the heart of her decision to go along with Dunya's plan of sacrificing herself for her brother's welfare. Pulkheria Alexandrovna clearly betrays her preference for her son by noting that Raskolnikov is even better looking than Dunya, when the reader knows that Dunya is a great beauty and that Raskolnikov must look rather haggard after his three days of high fever and unabated delirium. She is horrified at his abominable living quarters and cannot help noticing that he is more poorly dressed than the errand boy Vasya back home. She would like to rush and embrace him, but she understands that there is something strange about his behavior, and thus restrains herself for fear that Rodya's first sign of warmth will give way to his former surliness and hostility. Pulkheria's inner monologue is not a coherent argument, but a verbal rendering of the data of mood and sensation.

An especially good example that emphasizes the logical movement rather than the feel and flux of consciousness is Raskolnikov's reaction to his mother's letter. The quoted passage is a small part of a five-page-long interior monologue recording Raskolnikov's indignation at what appears to be his sister's decision to marry a man whom she does not love in order to further Raskolnikov's career. At this point Raskolnikov has not yet committed himself to the murder.

Why there's no denying that the Svidrigaylovs are difficult. It's no picnic to spend one's life roaming about the provinces as a governess for two hundred rubles, but I also know that my sister would rather be a Negro slave on a plantation or a Lettish serf in the employ of a Baltic German than defile her spirit and her moral sensibilities by a marriage with a man whom she does not respect and with whom she has nothing in common — and forever, solely for her own personal advantage. Even if Luzhin were the purest gold, a perfect diamond, even then she would not consent to become Mr. Luzhin's lawful concubine. Why then is she now consenting? Just what can the reason be? Where does the key to this riddle lie? It's quite clear, for herself, for her own comfort, even to save her own life, she would not sell herself, but for someone else, she would! For someone dear to her, for someone she adores, she would! That explains everything; for her brother, for her mother, she would sell herself! She would sell everything! Oh, in such circumstances, we overcome our moral feelings; we put everything up for sale: our freedom, our peace of mind; even our conscience. Our own lives be damned if only our beloved creatures are happy. Moreover, we invent a casuistry all of our own, we learn from the Jesuits, and for a time perhaps we lull our consciences and convince ourselves that it is necessary to act so, really necessary, in such a good cause. That is the way we are, and it's all as clear as daylight. (38)

Raskolnikov certainly appears more of a rhetorician and moralist in this passage than a potential murderer. The whole argument can be summed up in a sentence: although Dunya would never consent to sell herself to a man like Luzhin for her own personal advantage, she would for the sake of her mother and brother. The rest is rhetoric, undeniably highly charged and very effective, but rhetoric nevertheless. His description of what Dunya would do before selling herself to Luzhin for her own personal advantage is an obvious exaggeration: she would rather be a Negro slave on a plantation or a Lettish serf in the employ of a Baltic German

than marry such a man. In other words, Raskolnikov cannot believe that
she would bind herself forever in this way solely for her own personal
gain. Then he turns the attack around, suggesting ironically that even if
Luzhin were the purest gold, a perfect diamond, Dunya would still not
consent to be his legal concubine. It is obvious that Raskolnikov does
not think Luzhin is made of the purest gold. His use of such an expression, therefore, even in a hypothetical statement, is sarcastic hyperbole.

From the very first lines, it is clear that this monologue is not being
used to record the inchoate, formless flux of sensation and consciousness;
it is instead a strictly logical argument, effectively employing the devices
of classical rhetoric. The sentences are long, complex, and periodic, and
generally employ several degrees of logical subordination. The short
telegraphic phrases so characteristic of modern interior monologue are
conspicuously absent. The sentences are causally related and utilized to
produce a carefully calculated rhetorical effect. First Luzhin is compared
by implication to a merciless slaveowner. In the very next sentence he is
mentioned in connection with human perfection. Not only is each sentence an obvious hyperbole, but so is the juxtaposed contrast: he's an
inhuman despot; he's a paragon of virtue.

Though the rest of the quotation has a different structure, its tone is
the same. Exclamations, rhetorical questions, and emphatic repetition
abound. Raskolnikov begins by asking why Dunya is consenting to marry
Luzhin if she is not doing it for personal advantage. It is clearly a
rhetorical question, and so it is not surprising that he himself answers it
in detail. "It's quite clear, for herself, for her own comfort, even to save
her own life she would not sell herself, but for someone else, she would.
For someone dear to her, for someone she adores, she would! That
explains everything; for her brother, for her mother, she would sell herself! She would sell everything!" The repetition of the preposition "for"
in the sense of "for whose sake" is extremely effective here, because it
underlies the theme of the whole monologue: for whom is Dunya making
this great sacrifice? The same is true of the repetition of the verb "to
sell" — clearly a euphemism for prostitution. Raskolnikov has just heard
Marmeladov's story of how Sonya had become a prostitute in order to
help her family, and he cannot help making obvious comparisons. The
section ends with almost the same words as it begins: "it's all as clear as
daylight". The period has come full circle, the rhetorical question has
been asked and then logically and formally resolved.

The rhetoric in this passage, which is typical of the entire monologue,
is not accidental. Parallels and relationships essential to the thematic

structure of the novel are worked out in Raskolnikov's consciousness; between Marmeladov and himself; between Sonya and Dunya; between Katerina Ivanovna and Pulkheria Alexandrovna. Raskolnikov's awareness of these parallels may explain both his mental turmoil and his growing belief that murdering the pawnbroker is the only possible way of resolving his intolerable situation. Is Dunya, like Sonya Marmeladov, prostituting herself for her family? and is his mother, like Katerina Ivanovna, consenting to the sacrifice? Does that not mean that he is no better than the downtrodden and self-abasing Marmeladov; for, after all, he is the one who will profit from Dunya's shame. Has he not, like Marmeladov, brought about this sacrifice himself by refusing to support his indigent family? Raskolnikov's pride, above all, will not countenance such a sacrifice. To him, the letter is a clarion call to action: something must be done, and done quickly.

Though in this monologue Dostoevsky has focused essentially on the logic of consciousness, he nevertheless manages to convey a good deal of Raskolnikov's mental turmoil.[6] For the feel of Raskolnikov's consciousness here is also important. One must be moved by Raskolnikov's indignation, his anguish, and the stings of his wounded pride in order to understand the extremes to which he is willing to go to rectify his situation. Moreover, the narrator indicates that all these thoughts are not unfolding slowly and logically in Raskolnikov's brain; in fact, they are whirling through his head.

Other points in this long interior monologue, however, focus much more sharply on the emotive aspects of consciousness. One brief, but especially good, example occurs near the end, at a point where Raskolnikov has unalterably decided that he will on no account accept Dunya's sacrifice: "I don't want your sacrifice, Dunechka, I don't want it, mama! It won't happen while I'm alive. It won't, no it won't! I won't accept it." (39) Here the exclamations, short phrase units, emphatic repetition, and breakdown of the hypotactic syntax all effectively convey the rage, pain, and emotional turmoil Raskolnikov experiences while reading his mother's letter.

Interior monologue, however, does more than present the flux and logic of the characters' thoughts and emotions, it dramatizes them in such a way that they become at every moment crucial to the unfolding of the

---

[6] The emotional intensity of Dostoevsky's interior monologue, especially in contrast to Tolstoy's, is emphasized by M. N. Bojko, in "Vnutrennij monolog v proizvedenijax L. N. Tolstogo i F. M. Dostoevskogo," in *L. N. Tolstoj: Sbornik statej o tvorčestve*, ed. N. K. Gudzij (M.: Izd-vo Mosk. un-ta, 1959), pp. 83–99.

plot. One can get a better idea of how this is done by briefly contrasting the presentation of Raskolnikov's consciousness with that of the Underground Man.

Notes from the Underground, like *Crime and Punishment*, focuses almost exclusively on the consciousness of its hero. Yet though the dialectic process of argument and counterargument, which so epitomizes the Underground Man's consciousness, is itself dramatic, the very structure of the work precludes a dynamic and suspenseful interplay of action and consciousness, because Part One, the argument of *Notes from the Underground*, takes place sixteen years after the events in Part Two. It is essentially the Underground Man's attempt to give a philosophical explanation for his past and present behavior. But since what the Underground Man relates about his past is a reflection of his present understanding of that past, the action in Parts One and Two is not linked by cause and effect. The Underground Man's explanations in Part Two concerning his treatment of Liza are as much an aspect of his present consciousness as the monologue of Part One. There is unquestionably a direct relation in the work between consciousness and action, but Dostoevsky does not dramatize this relationship for psychological suspense. In fact, the exact opposite is the case. The Underground Man's position in Part One is brought about by his experiences in Part Two; they dissuade him from ever again becoming involved with other human beings. By having the events in Part Two motivate the confessions of Part One, Dostoevsky sacrifices to philosophical exegesis the suspense generated by presenting cause and effect in immediate juxtaposition and in chronological order.

In *Crime and Punishment*, by contrast, Raskolnikov's consciousness is always presented in direct relation to the events with which it is contemporaneous. Since Raskolnikov's thoughts and moods have a direct bearing on his actions, they play a crucial role in the development of the plot. Under such conditions, interior monologue becomes as instrumental in creating psychological suspense as some of the novel's more melodramatic coincidences and peripeties.

A good example of interior monologue building suspense comes from the passage discussed at the beginning of this chapter.

"... 'This purity, Dunechka, is indeed expensive!' And what if afterwards it becomes more than you can bear, and you regret it? How much grief and sorrow, how many curses, and how many tears hidden from everybody, because after all, you are not Marfa Petrovna. And what will become of mother? You know even now she is uneasy and worried; and how about when she sees everything clearly? And what of me? ... And just what have you taken me for? I don't want your sacrifice Dunechka, I don't want it, mama! It won't happen while I'm alive. It won't, no it won't! I won't accept it! " (39)

This section occurs at the very end of the monologue and thus represents the culminating point of the debate that rages within Raskolnikov in reaction to his mother's letter. The reader agrees with Raskolnikov that he must do something to break out of his intolerable situation. "Now something must be done, now, do you understand that?" (39) His mother will go blind, his sister will have lost her youth and the possibility of happiness. There is no more time for idle daydreaming. The dramatization of consciousness here is clearly as crucial a part of the plot as Raskolnikov's meeting with Marmeladov in the tavern and his learning that Lizaveta will not be at the pawnbroker's at eight o'clock on the ninth. Here the workings of consciousness take the place of external action at the dynamic center of the plot.

CHAPTER 5

NARRATED CONSCIOUSNESS AND
INTERIOR ANALYSIS

Interior monologue is undeniably the most striking and direct method of transcribing consciousness in *Crime and Punishment*.[1] It permits the greatest possible individualization of thought and feeling; it takes us into the deepest levels of consciousness; and because it is almost always developed at some length, it allows great latitude for presenting a consistent argument within a single passage. Yet it is used far less than narrated consciousness and interior analysis, for first-person narration, which is essential to render interior monologue, has serious limitations.

Despite Dostoevsky's skill in integrating it into the story, interior monologue cannot be expected to combine action, commentary, and the transcription of thoughts and perceptions as effectively as interior analysis or narrated consciousness. Interior monologue works remarkably well for scenes in which all the action is in the character's mind, like the one in which Raskolnikov reads his mother's letter. In this scene, though Raskolnikov is actually walking in the streets, he is oblivious to everything around him; nothing impinges upon his consciousness; he is totally wrapped up in the problems of his mother and sister. In other parts of the book, however, large sections of interior monologue would either seriously retard the action or prevent the relating of important events that go on while a character's consciousness is being recorded. Since the tense and person of interior monologue contrast with the surrounding

---

[1] For several representative works on third-person techniques of transcribing mental processes, see Bernhard Fehr, "Substitutionary Narration and Description," *English Studies*, 20 (1938), 97–107; Lawrence E. Bowling, "What is Stream of Consciousness Technique?" *PMLA*, 65 (1950), 341–5; Franz Stanzel, "Episches Praeteritum, erlebte Rede, historische Praesens," *Deutsche Vierteljahrsschrift für Literaturwissenschaft und Geistesgeschichte*, 32 (1959), 1–12; Dorrit Cohn, "Narrated Monologue: Denition of a Fictional Style," *Comparative Literature*, 18 (1966), 97–112; Ronald James Lethcoe, "Narrated Speech and Narrated Consciousness" (Unpublished Ph.D. Dissertation, Univ. of Wisconsin, 1969).

third-person narration, it calls attention to itself and thus tends to break the flow of events. This impression is further reinforced by its considerable length and its uninterrupted character.

Third-person techniques are much more effective at integrating consciousness and external action; they neither impede the flow of conversation nor defuse the tension of scenic episodes. Moreover, they contain some of the most significant examples of narrational commentary — a remarkable feature necessarily absent from all passages of interior monologue. Since there are also important differences between narrated consciousness and interior analysis in *Crime and Punishment*, they will be treated separately. Their interrelation, however, will not be neglected.

NARRATED CONSCIOUSNESS

Narrated consciousness is not a new technique. Though extensively practiced only in the twentieth century, it can be found in many nineteenth-century psychological novels. In fact, it may be employed in any third-person novel in which the narrator is not himself a character. The narrator may be subjective or omniscient, but far more often he is impersonal, or at least undramatized.

Narrated consciousness is composed of two distinct techniques: narrated speech and narrated perception. Narrated speech (*erlebte Rede*) reproduces a character's consciousness by presenting his thoughts and feelings as they might conceivably have been expressed in speech. Narrated perception, as its name implies, verbalizes perceptions and sensations. Unlike interior monologue, however, which uses the tenses of direct discourse, narrated consciousness uses those of indirect discourse. It also dispenses with introductory phrases of cognition and sensation, which commonly indicate interior analysis — a less direct way of presenting the characters' thoughts and perceptions. These differences can be seen in the following example:

interior monologue:	"I just don't care any more."
narrated consciousness (speech):	He just didn't care any more.
interior analysis:	He knew that he just didn't care any more.

In narrated consciousness, the tenses of direct speech are transformed into indirect speech. "I'll definitely go," becomes "He'd definitely go" — without, of course, the quotation marks.

The grammar of narrated consciousness is not its only distinguishing characteristic. Narrated speech, for example, can be easily identified by the presence of many words, expressions, and phrases which are associated with a certain character and which differ considerably from the narrator's prose. Expressions, such as "you know", "but", "well", "you see", and "really" are often reliable indicators of its presence. Russian differs somewhat from French, English, and German in that it can use either present or past tense for narrated consciousness. This gives Russian the possibility of creating effects very similar to interior monologue without sacrificing any of the advantages of narrated consciousness.[2]

The special way in which narrated consciousness integrates action, thought, and commentary can be well illustrated by a passage from Chapter Five, Part Five. The focus in this chapter is on the Marmeladovs and particularly on the pathetic spectacle of Katerina Ivanovna, half mad, on the streets of St. Petersburg. Very little of Raskolnikov's consciousness is recorded, and yet the reader must be informed of the hero's reactions to the tumultuous events of Part Five — Marmeladov's funeral feast and Raskolnikov's confession of the murder to Sonya. By using narrated consciousness Dostoevsky concisely and effectively transcribes Raskolnikov's feelings and thoughts without shifting the emphasis from Katerina Ivanovna.

Each sentence of the quoted passage is followed by a description, in brackets, of the specific technique employed, showing how Dostoevsky weaves in and out of the consciousness of his character.

Raskolnikov had not been listening for quite a while. [description of action] Reaching his house, he nodded to Lebezyatnikov and turned in at the gate. [description of action] Lebezyatnikov snapped to, looked around, and hurried on. [description of action]
   Raskolnikov went into his little room and stood still in the middle of it. [description of action] "Why had he returned here?" [narrated consciousness (speech)] He examined the yellow tattered wallpaper, the dust, the sofa. ... [description of perception] From the yard came a sharp continuous knocking: it was as though somewhere something was being hammered in, a nail perhaps. ... [narrated consciousness (perception)] He went up to the window, rose on his tiptoes [description

   [2] For the characteristics of narrated consciousness in Russian, see I. I. Kovtunova, "Nesobstvenno-prjamaja reč' v sovremennom russkom literaturnom jazkye," *Russkij jazyk v škole*, 14, No. 2 (1953), 18–27; L. A. Sokolova, *Nesobstvenno-avtorskaja (nesobstvenno-prjamaja) reč' kak stilističeskaja kategorija* (Tomsk: Izd. Tomskogo un-ta, 1968); Wolf Schmid, *Der Textaufbau in den Erzählungen Dostoevskijs* (Munich: Wilhelm Fink Verlag, 1973), pp. 52–60.

of action] and looked out into the yard for a long time with a look of rapt attention. [description of perception] But the yard was empty and he could not make out who was hammering. [narrated consciousness (perception)] In the wing on the left, here and there, he could see open windows; on the windowsills stood pots of sickly geraniums. [interior analysis and narrated consciousness (perception)] The wash was hung out of the windows. ... [narrated consciousness (perception)] He knew all this by heart. [interior analysis] He turned away and sat down on the sofa. [description of action]

Never, never before had he felt himself so frightfully alone! [narrated consciousness (speech)]

Yes, he felt once more that he would perhaps really come to hate Sonya, especially when he had made her more unhappy. [interior analysis verging on narrated consciousness (speech)]

"Why had he gone to her to beg her tears? [narrated consciousness (speech)] Why did he so need to torment her? [narrated consciousness (speech)] Oh, how base!" [narrated consciousness (speech)]

"I will remain alone," he said resolutely, "and she shall not come to the prison!" [interior monologue]

About five minutes later he raised his head with a strange smile. [description of action] He had a strange thought. [interior analysis]

"Perhaps it would really be better in Siberia." [interior monologue] (328)

The first four sentences of the quoted passage swiftly summarize Raskolnikov's departure from Lebezyatnikov and his return to his apartment. Having reached his garret, he asks himself why he has returned. The quotation marks around this question, phrased in the third person, clearly indicate that it is narrated speech. Although we have entered Raskolnikov's consciousness no sharp break has occurred in the narrative. Since narrated consciousness is unencumbered by introductory verbs of thinking or perception, and no change whatsoever need be made in tense or person, the transition between action and consciousness is as smooth as cinematic montage. Unlike French, German, and English, Russian does not even alternate past tenses. For these reasons, the shift in the next sentence from consciousness back to action is equally smooth: "He examined the yellow tattered wallpaper, the dust, the sofa. ..." By alternating action, interior analysis and narrated speech, the narrator is able to slip as effortlessly in and out of consciousness, as in the escape scene analyzed in Chapter Two, without either sacrificing psychological immediacy or disrupting the flow of the action.

Dostoevsky obviously chose to use narrated consciousness rather than interior monologue to avoid transferring the complete attention of the reader from the Marmeladovs to Raskolnikov, but he accomplished other purposes as well. Since in interior monologue the character whose consciousness is being transcribed is invariably lost in thought and oblivious to his surroundings, the reader feels — as he ought — bottled up inside the character. Few readers remember that the long passage of interior monologue recording Raskolnikov's reactions to his mother's letter was presented while he was walking the streets. "He walked as was his habit, without noticing his way, muttering and even speaking to himself, to the astonishment of the passers-by. Many of them took him to be drunk." (36) On the other hand, if narrated consciousness is the principal means of transcribing thoughts and feelings, the reader is very much aware of the physical world of the character. In fact he sees it through the character's eyes, hears it through the character's ears. So, in this section, in addition to following Raskolnikov's train of thought, we also see his physical environment as it is reflected in his consciousness and his consciousness as it is reflected in the sensations and objects that impinge on him from the outside world.

While ostensibly transcribing Raskolnikov's thoughts and perceptions, Dostoevsky uses these objects and sensations in the external world as symbols bearing on Raskolnikov's mental, physical, and spiritual condition. Since the perceptions are Raskolnikov's, the narrator does not appear responsible for the suggestive commentary which they harbor. Nor does the symbolism seem forced; one can easily interpret what Raskolnikov sees as the projection of his own despair.

Raskolnikov has just confessed the murder to Sonya, but the confession has scarcely lessened his suffering. Perhaps he thought he could rid himself of the incubus of the pawnbroker by telling everything to Sonya, but his release cannot be effected so quickly or simply. His inner need to confess is a sign that his whole constitution is rebelling against his nefarious deed. Confessing to Sonya is not enough; she is, in a sense, a criminal too, and he knows she will not reproach him. But he nevertheless uses her badly. He insults her, torments her with her intolerable position, and promises her nothing but further woe and degradation. At one point he is within an inch of murdering her — so much does she resemble the innocent Lizaveta — with her gentle and beautiful eyes full of the most childlike horror. From a moral point of view, Raskolnikov's confession is seriously flawed. He admits that he did the deed, but expresses neither remorse nor guilt. For he cannot accept that the murder of such a "noxious parasite" can be considered a crime. He leaves Sonya with his problems still essentially unresolved. She has sown the seed of hope in him, but it will be some time before the soil will be receptive.

Yet, for some reason, after the confession, Raskolnikov returns to his room. His question as to why he has returned there indicates that he is painfully aware of its physical and symbolic significance for his present situation. Its dust and cramp, its closeness and peeling yellow wallpaper cannot but remind him that his plans for the murder were first hatched here. It is the pervading symbol of his unbending pride and his willful isolation from his fellow man. He would rather rot in his garret than demean himself by working as do other students.

Since the room seems to underline his present dilemma, it can offer him little consolation or hope. Moreover, the depressing sights and sounds on the outside suggest that he sees as little hope beyond himself as within. At the height of summer the geraniums are dying. And the hammering seems like the noise of a coffin being closed by some invisible force, as though fate were shutting off the last avenues of escape. Or is what Raskolnikov perceives merely a projection of his consciousness, the ruminations of a seriously deteriorating organism? Does his jaundiced eye seek out the geranium, does the pounding in his head synchronize with the hammering of nails in the yard? Whatever may be the emotional, psychological, or symbolic implications of the imagery — and the ellipses here indicate that Dostoevsky is asking the reader to fill them in for himself — Raskolnikov's room and surroundings make us share his despondency and his dim but ominous forebodings. Raskolnikov turns away from the window and sits down on his sofa: "Never, never before had he felt himself so frightfully alone." His thought here merely echoes the visual, mental, and auditory images that we have shared with him during these last harrowing moments.

INTERIOR ANALYSIS

Interior analysis is the third major method that Dostoevsky employs to transcribe consciousness.[3] It is a much broader technique than narrated consciousness and it is found on almost every page of *Crime and Punishment*. It can present the point of view of either the character or the narrator, and sometimes, like narrated consciousness, it does both at the

---

[3] Bowling, pp. 341–4, and Cohn, pp. 104, 110, refer to this technique as internal analysis; Robert Humphrey, *Stream of Consciousness in the Modern Novel* (Berkeley: Univ. of California Press, 1954), pp. 29, 33–4, calls it indirect interior monologue; and Robert Scholes and Robert Kellogg, *The Nature of Narrative* (New York: Oxford Univ. Press, 1966), pp. 189, 190, 196, 198, label it narrative analysis.

same time. In interior analysis, however, the thoughts, perceptions, and emotions of a character are presented much less directly than they are in narrated consciousness. The narrator frequently summarizes the inner lives of his characters and employs his own words to describe them. And when he does use what may be interpreted as their language, he invariably sets it off by some introductory phrase of perception or cognition such as: he thought, he felt, he understood, he saw.

A good example of interior analysis is the introduction of Part Three, Chapter Two, which presents Razumikhin's ruminations on his behavior before Dunya and Pulkheria Alexandrovna on the previous night.

> Razumikhin woke up the next morning after seven, troubled and serious. Many new and unforeseen problems suddenly had arisen for him. He had never before even imagined that he would wake up this way. He remembered the previous day to the smallest detail, and he realized that something unusual had happened to him, that he had been overcome by an impression unlike anything he had known before. At the same time, he clearly recognized that the dream which had kindled his imagination was absolutely unrealizable — so unrealizable that he was even ashamed of it, and he quickly passed over to other more urgent cares and problems, inherited from that "thrice accursed yesterday". (163)

In this passage the narrator analyzes Razumikhin's emotions and describes what is going on in his mind. He neither reproduces Razumikhin's train of thought nor uses any of his words. He does not show Razumikhin serious and troubled, but tells us that this is the case, just as he tells us that Razumikhin was faced with several new problems when he woke up the next morning. The interior analysis here is a summary of mental and emotional processes.

In the rest of the paragraph the narrator switches to recording Razumikhin's thoughts. However, he uses his own, not Razumikhin's words. Furthermore, almost every sentence is introduced by a phrase or word of cognition: he realized that; he clearly recognized that; he never imagined that. Because mental processes are presented much less directly than they would be in either interior monologue or narrated consciousness, there is significantly less immediacy and dramatic impact; the reader is less emotionally involved in the character's mental turmoil.

In this passage, however, interior analysis has compensating advantages. It not only effectively sets the scene for the new chapter, but also serves as an ideal introduction to the passages following it, in which Dostoevsky employs a combination of interior monologue and narrated consciousness to explore Razumikhin's thoughts and feelings more dramatically and directly. Since up to this point Dostoevsky has not provided a direct inner view of any character but Raskolnikov, the introductory paragraph of interior analysis smooths the transition not only to another character's perspective but to a radically different point of view. It is with good reason that the only words of Razumikhin that the narrator quotes in the entire paragraph, "thrice accursed yesterday", come at the end: they lead directly into narrated consciousness and interior monologue.

In addition, interior analysis can often closely approximate the effects of narrated consciousness. In some instances, it is even difficult to tell where one technique leaves off and the other begins. This is especially true of passages like the one below, which presents Raskolnikov's re-actions to Sonya as she enters his room in the presence of his mother and sister.

> He immediately realized that his mother and sister already knew something from Luzhin's letter about a certain girl of "disreputable" behavior. He had just protested against Luzhin's slander and mentioned that he had only seen the girl once, when all of a sudden she herself walked in. He recalled also that he hadn't even protested against the expression: "of disreputable behavior". All this confusedly and quickly flashed through his head. But looking more closely at her, he suddenly saw that this creature was so humiliated that he suddenly felt sorry for her. When she made a movement to run away in terror — it was as though something turned over inside him. (184)

In the first sentence, the narrator speaks of Raskolnikov recalling that his mother and sister already knew about a "certain girl of 'disreputable' behavior". The statement is presented indirectly; the past tense and third-person pronoun are used along with an introductory verb of perception; it is certainly interior analysis. And yet unmistakable elements of Raskolnikov's speech are also present. The phrase "a certain girl of 'disreputable' behavior" seems to be Raskolnikov's mimicry of Luzhin's stilted reference to Sonya. Although the next sentence is more difficult to analyze, it can easily be interpreted as narrated speech — Raskolnikov's mental review of an awkward situation. This becomes apparent if the sentence is converted into interior monologue: "I just protested against Luzhin's slander, and mentioned that I saw the girl once, when all of a sudden she herself walks in." But the same sentence can also be interpreted as the narrator's summary. These are not mutually exclusive possibilities; narrated speech can often subtly insinuate itself into the action. In passages like these, however, there is always the danger of ascribing an observation to the narrator that belongs to the character, if one fails to differentiate between the narrator's report and narrated speech. Raskolnikov's mental and emotional reactions in the remaining sentences of the paragraph are clearly interior analysis.

Interior analysis, because it is essentially a statement of the narrator, can perform certain functions denied to both narrated consciousness and interior monologue. I have already mentioned its use in summarizing mental life. Just as important, especially in *Crime and Punishment*, is its use as a vehicle for commentary that can be specifically attributed to the narrator. This commentary will be discussed in detail in succeeding chapters, but it is important to show at this point how it can blend with and evolve out of interior analysis.

A subtle example of narrational commentary integrated into interior analysis can be seen in the following passage, which records Raskolnikov's feelings after he has given all of his money to help Katerina Ivanovna with her husband's funeral.

> He walked down quietly, without hurry, in a high fever, but not conscious of it, filled with a new overwhelming sensation of powerful full-blooded life welling up suddenly inside of him. This sensation might be compared to that of a man condemned to death who has unexpectedly been pardoned. Halfway down the staircase he was overtaken by the priest on his way home; silently Raskolnikov let him pass and exchanged a silent bow with him. When he was at the foot of the stairs, he heard hurried footsteps behind him. Someone was trying to overtake him: it was Polenka. She was running after him, calling "Wait! wait!" (146–7)

Raskolnikov leaves Katerina Ivanovna in a surprisingly more buoyant and sanguine mood than when he arrived. Just a few moments earlier his despair had become so intense that he had decided to go to the police station and confess everything. But his spontaneous act of generosity seems to free the forces of life imprisoned within him. In order to dramatize and make even more vivid Raskolnikov's feeling at this moment of apparent renewal, the narrator suggests a comparison that unmistakably, but subtly, reveals his own view of Raskolnikov's situation — that Raskolnikov is like a man condemned to death who suddenly and unexpectedly is pardoned. In this comparison, the narrator suggests that up to this point Raskolnikov's life has been a death in life, the life of a condemned man. His boundless rationalism and pride have made healthy relationships with other human beings impossible. His spontaneous and unreasoned act of generosity toward Katerina Ivanovna, however, seems to open up new hope, just as it fills him with a physical sensation of the seething forces of life. As in the epilogue, life takes the place of dialectics and gives promise of salvation and renewal. The narrator takes care to point out the absence of all rationality in Raskolnikov's experience: it is entirely emotional; it is sudden and unexpected; and it brings forth an almost mystical sense of well-being, the feeling of a condemned man miraculously snatched from death. The implications of this brief comparison are enormously important. It presents very early in the novel a possible solution to Raskolnikov's moral dilemma, and thus foreshadows the events of the epilogue. There is indeed still hope for Raskolnikov; it lies in the spontaneous, nonrational, and generous impulses of the heart.

That implications of such significance can be drawn from this comparison attests the effectiveness and flexibility of interior analysis in bringing the narrator's point of view to bear on our assessment of event and character. Yet it is one of the subtlest devices at the disposal of the author, for it does its work while transcribing consciousness. Moreover, by rendering consciousness so suggestively and poetically, Dostoevsky provides us with a different and perhaps richer means of understanding Raskolnikov's mental and spiritual life, while at the same time giving us the touchstone by which we may evaluate Raskolnikov's motives and deeds.

The commentary found in the interior analysis of Luzhin's consciousness is far more explicit and often distinctly sarcastic. The first few pages of Part Five present an especially good example. Luzhin has just suffered a severe setback in his effort to secure Raskolnikov's sister for his wife, and we see him still smarting from his recent discomfiture: "The black snake of wounded pride had been sucking at his heart all night" (279), states the narrator, leaving no doubt as to his opinion of the novel's most unappealing character. Though he generally lets Luzhin speak for himself, either in dialogue or interior monologue, at times he makes snide comments on Luzhin's motivation: "He was for staying with him [Lebezyatnikov] on his arrival in Petersburg not totally out of niggardly economy, although this, in fact, was almost the main reason, but there was also another reason." (281) There is no need to elaborate here on the nature of such commentary. Suffice it to say that it is typical of the stronger narrational commentary that we find in interior analysis, and it contrasts sharply with the low-keyed type used with Raskolnikov, and between these poles lie multitudinous gradations.

THE INTERRELATION OF NARRATED CONSCIOUSNESS AND INTERIOR ANALYSIS

Interior analysis has some important similarities to narrated consciousness. Indeed in some instances the two techniques overlap. Because of the presence of introductory words or phrases of perception and cognition, a passage shot through with the idiosyncrasies of a character's speech may, from a grammatical viewpoint, be classified as interior analysis, though in every other respect it would appear to be narrated consciousness, which invariably uses the speech patterns of the individual whose thought is being probed. In *Crime and Punishment*, few passages use either one technique or the other. In the vast majority of cases they either exist side by side or are thoroughly combined. In this way Dostoevsky is able to achieve optimal subtlety and effectiveness. The following passage, which demonstrates how the two techniques work together, also concerns Luzhin.

> In a word, he decided to try Petersburg. He knew that "much, very much" could be gained with a woman's help. The fascination of a charming, virtuous, and well-educated woman could singularly ease his way, attract attention to him, create an aura about him ... and now everything was ruined! This sudden terrible break had struck him like a lightning bolt. It was some sort of terrible joke, an absurdity! He had been a little bit overbearing; he hadn't even managed to say all he wanted, he had simply made a little joke, got carried away, but it ended so seriously! And after all he did really like Dunya in his own way, he already lorded it over her in his dreams — and suddenly! ... No! But tomorrow, tomorrow, all this had to be set right, patched up, corrected, but most important of all — he had to destroy that impudent snot-nosed brat, the cause of the whole thing. With a pained sensation he recalled also involuntarily Razumikhin ... but, on that score, however, he was easy. "As if such a boy could be put on his level." The one whom he was really afraid of was Svidrigaylov. ... In a word, a great deal of trouble still lay ahead. ... (238)

In this passage the narrator explores Luzhin's consciousness after his mortifying meeting in Part Four with Razumikhin and Raskolnikov's family. He played the bully and it backfired. Dunya and her mother turned against him, and Razumikhin was a hair's breadth from throwing him down the stairs. The loss of Dunya was an especially cruel blow for him, because he really liked her; and even more important, she was essential to his career. Basically an uncultured and poorly educated pettifogger from the provinces, Luzhin believed a sophisticated and charming wife was necessary to smooth his way into influential circles.

The paragraph begins with the narrator's summing up Luzhin's reasons for coming to Petersburg. He then reports in indirect statement — but using some of Luzhin's own words — that women could be of great help to him. It seems it is the narrator who says that the "terrible" (*bezo-braznyj*) break acted on Luzhin like a lightning bolt, but the Russian word *bezobraznyj* might just as well be attributed to Luzhin, for it is so used in the following sentence, which clearly is narrated speech: "It was some sort of terrible joke, an absurdity!" Narrated speech continues unabated for several sentences, but incorporated within are obvious elements of the narrator's critical commentary. "And after all he did really like Dunya in his own way, he already lorded it over her in his dreams — and suddenly!" The narrator's qualifying phrase, "in his own way", certainly disabuses us of any favorable impression we may have had of Luzhin's feelings for Dunya. Even his animal attraction to Dunya is no more than a desire to dominate her for the purpose of inflating his own ego. Slipping back into interior analysis, the narrator subtly indicates that Luzhin's dismissal of Razumikhin as unworthy of consideration is indeed a serious miscalculation. "But, on that score, however, he was easy." Gradually the narrator slips entirely out of Luzhin's consciousness and rounds off the paragraph with the same ironic phrase that he used to conclude a previous section: "In a word." Of course, the narrator has said more than a word; his formulation that Luzhin has a lot of problems on his hands is ironic understatement.

What then are the effects in this passage of alternating narrated consciousness and interior analysis? For one, the smoothness with which the narrator slips from one technique to the other guarantees that no sharp break occurs in the report of consciousness. Despite the heterogeneity of this material, the reader feels as though he is closely following the character's thoughts and feelings without interruption. Moreover, the narrator's consistent use of the character's own words in recording consciousness creates the impression of an intimacy comparable to that which we find in interior monologue. Though the combination of interior analysis and narrated consciousness cannot reproduce the psychic processes in their logical development as effectively as interior monologue, it has compensating advantages. It speeds up the narrative line significantly and permits the narrator to insert his own remarks, without either interrupting the flow of consciousness or calling attention to his person.

The transcription of consciousness is a complex literary phenomenon. The techniques for rendering mental life, however, are far from being the exclusive property of select twentieth-century novelists. Although Dostoevsky did not write stream of consciousness novels, he was compelled by his unique artistic vision to make use of all the techniques of recording mental life at his disposal. Fully understanding the ultimate incommensurability of literary language and "raw" consciousness, Dostoevsky was not afraid to use the narrator to bridge the gap between the reality of conscious life and the demands of his reader, if by doing so he could give a richer and more complete picture of that psychological world which was his alone.

CHAPTER 6

BRIEF NARRATIONAL COMMENTARY

The narrator in *Crime and Punishment* is not nearly so impersonal as many critics in the past have assumed.[1] Though not a character in the novel in the sense that Raskolnikov and Sonya are, he nevertheless plays a crucial role in structuring our perception. His point of view colors every act and thought. It is manifest in interior analysis and it often insinuates itself into narrated consciousness. Ultimately, it governs our interpretations of all the events and characters and underpins the evaluative norms of the entire novel. The world of *Crime and Punishment*, after all, is governed by very definite poetical laws, and it is the narrator's role constantly to impress upon the reader their importance and validity.

Thus the narrator of *Crime and Punishment* is in many ways a personality. True, we cannot see him; but since so much of the novel is filtered through his mind's eye, we willy-nilly, by novel's end, come to know him rather well. His likes and dislikes and the moral standards by which he measures the characters and their actions are evident in all his commentary. Sometimes he states his opinions subtly, but at other times he can be rather heavy-handed. Although many readers have viewed the narrator's comments in *Crime and Punishment* as an artistic defect, an examination of their use shows that they are always appropriate and at times even essential to the narrative.[2]

The narrator employs many different methods for injecting his commentary into the novel. Sometimes he is brief, using a mere epithet or an

---

[1] For a representative list of those who have argued that the narrator is impersonal and objective, see Note 4 in Chapter One.

[2] A good example of a critic who disparages the narrator's use of strong commentary in *Crime and Punishment* is J. M. Meijer, "Situation Rhyme in a Novel of Dostoevsky," in *Dutch Contributions to the Fourth International Congress of Slavicists* (The Hague: Mouton, 1958), p. 117.

ironic phrase. At other times he stops the action to give an extended opinion. His commentary may be so subtle — low-keyed and unobtrusive — that in some cases it is difficult to tell that he is, in fact, voicing an opinion. Or it may be what twentieth-century objectivist critics call heavy-handed or obtrusive — terms that reflect their negative attitude toward personalized narrators. It can further be direct and/or indirect depending upon who is the object of the commentary. (The narrator's comments on Luzhin's character, for example, are direct with reference to Luzhin, but to the extent that they reveal something about Raskolnikov, whether he is specifically mentioned or not, they are also indirect.) And of course they can be explicit, stating in no uncertain terms what the narrator thinks, as, for example, when he calls Lebezyatnikov an ignoramus, or implicit, making a point through metaphor, irony, or merely the connotation of a word.

Moreover, the narrator may use these techniques in various combinations. Implicit commentary may range from extreme subtlety to blunt periphrasis. And even the briefest comment may be direct and indirect, subtle or heavy-handed, explicit or implicit. It is the narrator's brief commentary, and the variety of ways it is employed, that I shall examine in this chapter.

One of the strongest forms of brief commentary is the evaluative epithet. In the scene in which Sonya reads to Raskolnikov about Lazarus' rising from the dead, we find a passage where the narrator openly reveals his sympathy for Sonya's religious beliefs: "'This is all about the raising of Lazarus,' she whispered sternly and abruptly, and turning away she stood motionless, not daring, almost ashamed, to raise her eyes to him. Her feverish trembling continued. The candle had long since reached its end in the twisted candlestick, dimly illuminating in the poverty-stricken room the murderer and the harlot, who had so strangely come together to read the Eternal Book. Five minutes or more passed." (254)

This evaluative formula — the murderer and the harlot strangely coming together to read the Eternal Book — has a clearly rhetorical ring. The word *bludnica* (harlot) is a strictly ecclesiastical term, and it is apparent that the narrator uses it here in preference to the more secular *prostitutka* (prostitute). *Bludnica* immediately links Sonya with Mary Magdalene; for despite the corruption of the flesh, Sonya too has remained spiritually pure; in a world of doubting Thomases, she has preserved her faith. Merely by referring to the Bible as the Eternal Book, the narrator reveals that he embraces its truth and by implication Lazarus' resurrection. Consequently, he not only takes Sonya's side in the struggle with Raskolnikov's demonic pride, but clearly shares Sonya's faith that Raskolnikov, like Lazarus, may rise from the dead. The importance of this passage can hardly be overestimated; it gives substance to Sonya's belief and provides the reader with an important key to the novel's religious and philosophical presuppositions. Moreover, like the interior analysis in which Raskolnikov is compared to a man condemned to death who has unexpectedly been pardoned, this passage subtly foreshadows Raskolnikov's resurrection in the epilogue.

The narrator's statement here is not a violation of the novel's tone. In fact, the narrator's choice of words is perfectly in tune with the drama that is being played out before our eyes. Raskolnikov begins by tormenting Sonya with the inevitability of her destruction and the uselessness of sacrificing herself for the children. He then proceeds to question her faith in God. But strangest of all, he asks her to read to him the story of Lazarus' resurrection from the dead. Only after Sonya finishes reading several verses, does the narrator comment on this strange meeting of murderer and harlot over the Eternal Book. The narrator's statement does not jump out at the reader; on the contrary, it fuses with the elevated and explicit Biblical prose. Yet at the same time, it effectively describes the feverishness of the characters' emotions and the uniqueness of their fateful encounter. It is both the climax of the scene and a turning point in the novel; for it is Raskolnikov's first encounter with hope. It is thus fitting that the narrator rivet our attention on this moment. Five minutes of silence elapse after Sonya finishes reading, and in this brief interval the direction of Raskolnikov's life is completely changed.

The narrator's use of the word "harlot" in this scene is striking in still another way. It is strangely out of tune with his otherwise Victorian language in regard to sexual matters. When he is compelled elsewhere to discuss or describe Sonya's profession, he resorts to the standard euphemisms, as in his description of her arrival at the Marmeladovs' to see her dying father: "She was also in rags: her attire was extremely cheap, but done up in the fashion of the street, according to the taste and rules established in her special world, its purpose shamefully obvious." (144) At other times prostitutes are referred to as girls living by their own means, and whorehouses as "those well-known institutions". (8) The narrator's attitude toward prostitution, however, does not in all respects correspond to his primness in vocabulary. He obviously regards it as a social evil, but pities rather than condemns its practitioners. And he likes Razumikhin no less for regularly frequenting houses of ill-repute.

Another type of commentary in *Crime and Punishment*, very similar to the evaluative epithet, but far more frequently used, is the evaluative generalization. The narrator almost always reveals himself in such formulations, and often in what appear to be irrelevant statements lie important keys to the novel's most perplexing scenes. What, for example, could be more innocuous than the following statement about the weather in St. Petersburg?

> On the street the heat was frightful, added to this the stuffiness, the jostling, and the ubiquitous plaster, scaffolding, bricks, dust, and that special stench of summer, so familiar to every resident of Petersburg unable to procure a place in the country — all that had an immediate effect on the already frayed nerves of the youth. The insufferable stench from the taverns so numerous in this part of the city, and the drunks whom one met at every turn despite it being a working day, completed the revolting and depressing picture. (8)

The narrator's description of summer in Petersburg suggests that he is familiar with the stench of Petersburg summers because he too, at times, has not been fortunate enough to rent a place in the country. But the narrator's commentary does much more than personalize the locale; paradoxically, it gives it objectivity. For, by inserting his own comment, he assures us that this is not the distorted idea of the overwrought Raskolnikov, but a realistic description. He even enumerates the particulars that make the neighborhood so insufferable. It is a slum, and the narrator forthrightly brands it as depressing and repulsive. His obvious dislike of Petersburg is thus felt early in the novel. It is a concrete evil force with which Raskolnikov must contend. Like the drunkards in the taverns, indeed like Marmeladov himself, Raskolnikov will fall victim to its temptations and poisons.

Although, of course, not all generalizations are as strong as the one on Petersburg summers, many that at first seem purely descriptive, on closer inspection, reveal important commentary. Such, for example, is Raskolnikov's first impression of Marmeladov: "Sometimes we meet complete strangers whom we take an interest in at the first glance, suddenly, instantaneously, before a word is spoken. Such was the impression made on Raskolnikov by the person sitting next to him, who looked like a retired clerk." (14) In this generalization, the narrator can be said to have covered his tracks, for he unequivocally ascribes the impression to Raskolnikov. Nevertheless, the very fact that the narrator formulates Raskolnikov's thought with the help of a generalization makes it stand out in the text and take on far greater implications than it would at first seem to merit. Perhaps Raskolnikov is attracted to Marmeladov because he instinctively feels that he has something in common with him. (Raskolnikov's similar experience with Svidrigaylov later in the novel shows that such impressions can be quite accurate.) The commentary here is subtle and implicit. The narrator uses a generalization which ostensibly records Raskolnikov's consciousness to make the reader actively consider, throughout the monologue, the similarities between Marmeladov and Raskolnikov.

Some generalizations call attention to the basic themes, while others serve only to clarify a situation or to make an episode more vivid. Contrary to what one might expect, there does not seem to be any correlation between length and importance. Of the two generalizations quoted below, the shorter, the second, is of obviously greater significance.

Her cough began to choke her — but her warning proved effective. Evidently they were even considerably afraid of Katerina Ivanovna; *the tenants one after the other pressed back to the door with that strange inner sensation of satisfaction that always can be observed, among even those closest to a person overcome by misfortune, and from which without exception no one is spared, despite the sincerest compassion and sympathy.* (141) (Italics mine.)

It would have been difficult to sink any lower or let oneself go further; but in his present mental condition Raskolnikov found this even pleasing. He had completely secluded himself from everyone, like a tortoise in its shell, and even the face of the servant girl, who was obliged to wait upon him and who would sometimes look in on him, caused him to cringe with convulsive anger. *This often happens with certain monomaniacs, who have been excessively concentrating on something.* (26) (Italics mine.)

The first generalization, concerning the coexistence of sympathy and satisfaction at one's neighbor's misfortune, is purely descriptive. It does not appreciably add to our understanding of the Marmeladovs and has no bearing on Raskolnikov. It does, however, make the scene more vivid. By describing the feelings of the crowd as they leave the Marmeladovs' apartment, the narrator makes us party to what has happened; for we too have experienced the same selfish satisfaction in the presence of death.

The generalization concerning Raskolnikov's monomania has far greater implications. The narrator does not specifically call Raskolnikov a monomaniac, but he likens aspects of his behavior to one, and thus suggests the possibility. The comparison certainly implies that Raskolnikov has become excessively preoccupied with a single idea; but a definite connotation of insanity is also present; and this is a connotation of great significance, for it suggests that Raskolnikov's physical and mental deterioration and his inability even to tolerate the presence of other human beings are directly attributable to his noxious ideas — that Raskolnikov's condition is not so much the cause of his warped thinking as the logical result. The evaluative generalization, though brief, is one of the narrator's most effective and powerful tools.[3]

Perhaps the most diverse form of brief commentary is the ironic word or phrase. Some of the subtler uses of this device to deflate Raskolnikov's pretensions and undercut his moral position are discussed in Chapter Two. When used with other characters, however, the irony becomes far less subtle. In places, especially when directed at Luzhin and Lebezyatnikov, it borders on sarcasm. Katerina Ivanovna, though not subjected to the same rough treatment, nevertheless does not get off lightly; for the narrator has a special aversion to all forms of vanity and pretentiousness and simply will not permit them to strut about unchecked. We can better assess the nature and purpose of such commentary by briefly examining several passages typical of Dostoevsky's method.

Luzhin is probably the only character in the novel for whom Dostoevsky has no sympathy at all, and thus it is not surprising that he should be treated so harshly. In fact, Dostoevsky seems to create situations for the specific purpose of enabling the narrator to dissect Luzhin's motives and expose his vanity. A particularly good example occurs in Chapter One, Part Five, in which the narrator presents Luzhin's state of mind after his fateful interview with Dunya and Pulkheria Alexandrovna. Through four pages of interior monologue and interior analysis, Luzhin lambasts himself for his niggardly treatment of Dunya and her mother. "Had I spent some fifteen hundred rubles for the dowry, for example, for gifts, fancy little boxes, dressing cases, jewelry, fabric, and all that rubbish from Knopp's and the English store, then my position would have been better and ... stronger!" (280) Of course, Luzhin is really taking himself to task not for his stinginess, but for his miscalculation. All his thoughts reveal the meanness of his mind and his despicable values. It would seem that Luzhin has argued well enough against his own case, and commentary would be superfluous, but after he concludes his monologue with the

---

[3] For other generalizations, see *CP*, pp. 15, 27, 46–7, 115, 139, 171, 195, 230, 292, 346, 395, 396.

admission that he blundered, the narrator sees fit to add that after "Grinding his teeth again, Peter Petrovich called himself a fool — but not aloud, of course." (280) However uncalled for this jibe may seem at first, it serves an important purpose. Its effect is not so much to criticize Luzhin's vanity, that is, his fear of admitting his stupidity in the presence of others (it is implied that Lebezyatnikov is not only present but observing Luzhin quite closely), but to lower the tone of the whole passage. Luzhin's thoughts are damning, but they nevertheless constitute a sort of rhetorical argument. By employing such low humor, the narrator deflates the seriousness of Luzhin's deliberations and negates whatever rhetorical force they possess. The measure of Luzhin's consciousness is thus reflected in the tone of the narrative.

The narrator harps on Luzhin's vanity throughout the chapter. "It may be noted, by the way, that Peter Petrovich during the last week and a half willingly accepted (especially at the beginning) the strangest praise from Andrey Semenovich, that is he remained silent and made no objection, for instance, when Andrey Semenovich ascribed to him a readiness to further the speedy establishment of the new '*commune*', somewhere on Meshchansky Street, or not to interfere with Dunya if after a month of marriage she thought she might take a lover, or not to baptize his future children, and so on, all in the same vein. Peter Petrovich, as was his custom, did not object to the virtues ascribed to him, and even allowed himself to be praised for them — such was the pleasure he received from the most questionable type of praise." (282) The narrator's amusement at Luzhin's expense is much closer to sarcasm than to irony. Moreover, he adds insult to injury by describing the praise that Luzhin lapped up so unprotestingly — praise personally, and even ideologically, repugnant to Luzhin. The commune, representing the abolition of private property and the sharing of wealth, is the very antithesis of Luzhin's program of self-aggrandizement. Although obviously not Christian in the idealistic sense, Luzhin would never abstain from baptizing his children; it would ruin his career. But most astonishing is that Luzhin could calmly accept praise for being ready to let Dunya take a lover, for all his actions are motivated by his desire to possess Dunya, to be her sole master. The narrator's use of the word "strange" for this praise is a deliberate understatement, and thus all the more damning. Luzhin's vanity must indeed be great if he accepts as praise what we expect him to receive as the most flagrant of insults. The narrator registers not only his censure, but also his disgust. Though the commentary is not explicit, it is certainly powerful.

Endless seem to be the forms of irony the narrator employs to undercut Luzhin's vanity and self-satisfaction. Here they are exposed by the subtle use of narrated consciousness.

Having gotten out of bed Peter Petrovich immediately looked into the mirror. He feared that after the night he might look bilious. But on that score, at least for the time being, everything was fine, and having looked at his pale, noble face, which had grown somewhat fat of late, Peter Petrovich was for a moment consoled by the profound belief that he would find himself a bride somewhere else, and perhaps even a better one. (279)

Because it is incorporated into the transcription of consciousness, the narrator's commentary in this passage is not so obvious as in some of his other vicious sallies against Luzhin. But a close examination shows that the narrator is actually mimicking Luzhin for satiric effect. Luzhin looks at his noble pale countenance, which had grown fat of late, and assures himself that he is still capable of finding an even better catch than Dunya. The adjective "noble" must represent Luzhin's perception of himself, since it is cited as the reason for his belief that he can find someone to take Dunya's place — an opinion that the narrator does not share. But the very next phrase, stating that Luzhin's countenance had grown fat of late, seems to represent the narrator's perception, not Luzhin's. The Russian term used here is highly unflattering, and we thus cannot picture Luzhin using it to describe himself. Nor would such a perception lead him to believe he could easily find another girl. Because Luzhin's consciousness is presented partly from the narrator's point of view, the whole passage takes on the imprint of the narrator's irony. And the irony gradually becomes more insistent and depreciatory; everything about Luzhin is either mediocre or base.

The narrator also misses few opportunities to make ironic and often derogatory remarks about Katerina Ivanovna's misplaced vanity and overweening pride. In general, Dostoevsky's ironic treatment of Katerina Ivanovna is all of a piece, and any of a number of selections could have been chosen to demonstrate his method in puncturing her pretensions. The following report of Katerina Ivanovna's tirade at her husband's funeral feast is a particularly good example.

The older and more respectable of them, as though on purpose, as though they arranged it amongst themselves, all stayed away. Peter Petrovich Luzhin, for example, the most respectable, one might say, of the lodgers, didn't appear, and yet, only yesterday evening Katerina Ivanovna had succeeded in telling the whole world, that is Amalia Ivanovna, Polechka, Sonya, and the little Pole, that this most noble and magnanimous man, a man with the most influential connections and great fortune, a former friend of her first husband and who was received in her father's house, had promised to use all his means to obtain her a considerable pension. (294)

It will be noticed immediately that this passage is strikingly similar, as far as technique is concerned, to the one in which the narrator mimics Luzhin's words for ironic effect. It clearly presents Katerina Ivanovna's point of view: it is she who sees the absence of the older and more respectable guests as a conspiracy against her and makes a point of singling out Luzhin as the most respectable of all the lodgers. Yet, whereas most of the words are Katerina Ivanovna's, they are not merely reported; rather, they are incorporated into the narrator's summary and openly used against her. No sooner has Katerina Ivanovna started to multiply her inventions to present herself in a better light, than the narrator inserts a phrase that destroys her house of cards. "Katerina Ivanovna had succeeded in telling the whole world, that is Amalia Ivanovna, Polechka, Sonya, and the little Pole." The narrator calls direct attention to only one of Katerina Ivanovna's exaggerations, but by doing so he calls attention to them all. He thus undermines her pretensions at the very moment that she is flaunting them. Katerina Ivanovna is certainly a pathetic figure, and Dostoevsky shows compassion for her; but her foibles must be exposed. For she is as much a victim of pride as Raskolnikov; she too thinks she is better than other people. Her vanity plays a large part in Marmeladov's ruin, Sonya's degradation, and the suffering of her own children.

The least subtle form of irony found in *Crime and Punishment* is antiphrasis. Although genuine heavy-handed examples of this device — so commonly found in the works of Dickens, Balzac, and Gogol — are rather rare in *Crime and Punishment*, they nevertheless do exist. Antiphrasis discredits by dealing out undeserved compliments and respect to characters who unmistakably personify the exact opposite of the virtues attributed to them. Usually some disreputable or drunken figure is referred to as the honorable Mr. So-and-so — we all remember the honorable Mr. Bumble in *Oliver Twist*. A relatively unobtrusive instance of this technique in *Crime and Punishment* is the narrator's use of the word "noble" in his description of Luzhin. A more heavy-handed example is his description in Part One of Louisa Ivanovna being rebuked by the irascible assistant district inspector for a series of disturbances that recently occurred in her brothel. "As for the extravagantly dressed lady, at first she simply began to shudder from the thunder and lightning; but it was strange the more numerous and stronger the oaths became, the more amiable became her look, the more capitivating became her smile directed at the thundering lieutenant. She was mincing in place and continually curtseying, waiting impatiently for the time when she would finally be permitted to inject a word." (80) This passage alone to be sure does not make plain the narrator's ironic attitude toward Louisa Ivanovna. When viewed in the context of several previous descriptions of her person, however, such adjectives as "amiable" and "captivating" become obviously ironic and even amusingly risqué. Louisa Ivanovna is an obese woman, reeking of cheap perfume. She is wearing a light-blue balloon-like dress with white trimming; it spreads so fully around her chair that, according to the narrator, it takes up nearly half the room. Though she tries to look timid and self-effacing, she cannot conceal her impudent smile. The narrator dwells on these details throughout the scene. Knowing who she is and what she looks like, the reader may perceive her smile to be repulsive or even lewd; it is certainly neither charming nor captivating. Thus the irony here is obvious in the context of the novel. It is also well integrated. Louisa is not smiling captivatingly, but the narrator implies that she is consciously trying her best to do so. Dostoevsky is weaving commentary and description into a very tightly knit web: the antiphrasis in the novel is ingeniously toned down by having a functional purpose as well as an evaluative one.

As all these examples show, brief commentary is an efficient and economical narrative technique. A word, a phrase, or at most a sentence can have a considerable effect on the reader's interpretation of lengthy passages. Though used equally for minor and major characters, brief commentary is generally much more subtle when applied to Raskolnikov. This enables Dostoevsky to deepen the reader's understanding of his hero without significantly detracting from his dramatic presentation.

CHAPTER 7

EXTENDED NARRATIONAL COMMENTARY

In contrast to brief commentary, which is usually implicit, extended commentary is invariably explicit. Yet since its primary purpose is to throw light on a character different from the one at whom it is ostensibly aimed, it too harbors a great deal of implicit criticism. For although Raskolnikov is not, in the novel proper, the subject of extended commentary, he is, in most instances, its object. When the narrator analyzes Razumikhin's character, for example, he is essentially making a statement about Raskolnikov. In this way extended narrational commentary enables the narrator to evaluate his hero while focusing on a secondary figure. Sometimes the narrator employs positive commentary, sometimes negative. The effect is the same.

The most outstanding example of negative extended commentary is the introduction to Lebezyatnikov. Here the narrator lets loose a barrage of invective, innuendo, and insult that makes all the passages we have examined so far look tame by comparison.

This Andrey Semenovich was a cachectic, scrofulous, short fellow who served in some ministry. He had peculiarly flaxen hair and sported muttonchop whiskers of which he was very proud. Moreover, he constantly had trouble with his eyes. He was kindhearted enough, but his particularly self-assured speech always turned out to be ridiculously incongruous with his small size. But at Amalia Ivanovna's he was considered to be among the most respectable tenants; that is he didn't get drunk and paid his rent punctually. Despite all these qualities, Andrey Semenovich was really rather stupid. He aligned himself, however, with progress and "our younger generation" — from enthusiasm. He was one of that innumerable and varied legion of vulgarians, sickly nonentities, and willful ignoramuses who without fail instantly attach themselves to the most fashionable current idea only immediately to vulgarize it and instantly to caricature everything which they serve, however sincerely. (282)

The narrator begins his description with an attack on Lebezyatnikov's appearance. He is a scrofulous fellow of small stature, with peculiarly blond hair and poor eyesight, and he seems to be especially proud of his muttonchop whiskers. The disparity between his arrogant speech and his unimpressive appearance, the narrator tells us, nearly always makes him look ridiculous. His greatest claim to distinction is that he pays his rent punctually and drinks moderately. Though this is rather strong criticism, it is but a preamble to the caricature that follows. "Despite all these qualities," the narrator says, "Andrey Semenovich was really rather stupid." The antiphrasis is obvious; and the non sequitur in the last part of the sentence is brilliant and outrageous. We are fooled by the preposition "despite" into expecting the exact opposite conclusion. And yet the logical absurdity of the description is in tune with the ridiculousness of Lebezyatnikov's character. It is, if you will, a stylistic objective correlative. Moreover, the last sentence is a fitting conclusion to all that has preceded. It is perhaps the most explicit commentary in the novel. Nowhere else has the narrator packed as many evaluative epithets and nouns into one sentence. Lebezyatnikov is effectively labeled a vulgarian, a nonentity, and a willful ignoramus, who caricatures every idea to which he attaches himself.

Although this passage is unquestionably depreciatory, the narrator does not completely ignore Lebezyatnikov's positive side. He concedes that Andrey Semenovich is rather kindhearted; and the novel corroborates him on this point. At Marmeladov's funeral feast, Lebezyatnikov, following his heart, goes against his principles, first by approving of Luzhin's charity to Sonya, and then by exonerating her when she is falsely accused by her former "benefactor". Dostoevsky does not as a rule spring complete surprises with regard to characterization. In the end, the careful reader is rewarded.

But what is the function of the negative commentary in this passage? What does Dostoevsky gain by having the narrator disparage Lebezyatnikov's meager achievements? On the most obvious level, this description of Lebezyatnikov prepares the reader for his later tirades, thus making any additional comments unnecessary. But Soviet critics maintain that Dostoevsky uses Lebezyatnikov solely for the purpose of vilifying the political, social, and economic views of the radical intelligentsia. They point with some justice to Dostoevsky's polemic directed against Chernyshevsky[1] carried on in *Notes from the Underground*, where the hero

---

[1] A prominent Russian radical critic whose utopian socialistic novel, *What Is to Be Done?* (*Čto delat'?*), became a bible for a generation of Russian radicals and

lashes out at the radicals' ideas on science, the organization of society, human motivation, and free will. It was to continue to discredit these radical ideas, according to this argument, that Dostoevsky caricatured them in the person of the ridiculous, stupid, and unprepossessing Lebezyatnikov.[2]

Though one cannot categorically deny the Soviet point of view, we should be wary of viewing any of Dostoevsky's characters in purely propagandistic terms. To be sure, Dostoevsky is using Lebezyatnikov for his own ideological purposes; but the same may be said for all the characters in *Crime and Punishment* — Raskolnikov and Sonya are no less reflections of his ideological position than is Lebezyatnikov. And even Lebezyatnikov is not the straw man that Soviet critics have made him out to be. The focus of the narrator's attacks on Lebezyatnikov is not so much the radical social theories of the time, but their vulgarization by pretentious nonentities. He does not judge the ideas themselves. The very fact that Lebezyatnikov vulgarizes them would seem to enhance rather than detract from their worth in the eyes of the reader. But if Lebezyatnikov represents the ideas of the younger generation at their most ridiculous, he also represents them at their most harmless. For the narrator, the Lebezyatnikovs of Russian society pose no real and present danger. Fortunately, they are not totally committed to their half-baked ideas, as Lebezyatnikov's later "retrogressive" vindication of Sonya clearly demonstrates. (He could have argued, like Raskolnikov, that a certain percentage of the world's Sonyas had to be sacrificed every year for the good of society.) And indeed Dostoevsky's arguments against the radical ideas of the younger generation would have had little impact had they culminated in the portrayal of Lebezyatnikov. The real significance of this passage is that it provides indirect commentary on several more important characters who hold very similar ideas.

The ideas of self-interest preached by the younger generation are presented as ridiculous when vulgarized by harmless ignoramuses like Lebezyatnikov, but frighteningly destructive when taken to their logical extremes in the real world by the more aggressive, self-seeking, and intellectually gifted. The ludicrousness of Lebezyatnikov's distortion of radical ideas highlights, by contrast, the real life consequences of these

---

revolutionaries, and a main object of attack in Dostoevsky's *Notes from the Underground* and *Crime and Punishment*.

[2] See, for example, N. M. Čirkov, *O stile Dostoevskogo* (M.: AN SSSR, 1967), pp. 110–12; V. Ja. Kirpotin, *Razočarovanie i krušenie Rodiona Raskol'nikova* (M.: Sov. pisatel', 1972), pp. 256–66.

theories in the deeds of Svidrigaylov, Luzhin, and Raskolnikov. Lebezyatnikov's good heart prevents him from following his convictions; but Luzhin, Svidrigaylov, and Raskolnikov no longer possess such a sure defense against their aggressive instincts; they do not swerve in their pursuit of their own self-interest. Dostoevsky's use of invective in the above passage then is essentially indirect: its real target is not so much Lebezyatnikov, or even Chernyshevsky, but Raskolnikov and his foils.

The narrator in *Crime and Punishment* also makes considerable use of positive extended commentary. Most, but not all, of it concerns Pulkheria Alexandrovna and Razumikhin. The passages that will be discussed here are, like the one dealing with Lebezyatnikov, of paragraph length, explicit, and replete with indirect criticism of Raskolnikov. The first passage is the encomium to Raskolnikov's mother in Part Three, Chapter Two. Pulkheria Alexandrovna and her daughter Dunya have just arrived in Petersburg only to find their darling Rodya irritable, ill, and openly hostile. Razumikhin manages to persuade them to leave Raskolnikov and visit him on the following day. After Razumikhin conducts them to their hotel room, the narrator takes the opportunity to say a few words about Pulkheria Alexandrovna:

> Although Pulkheria Alexandrovna was forty-three, her face still preserved traces of its former beauty; and what is more she seemed much younger than her years, which is almost always the case with women who have preserved into old age a clarity of mind, a freshness of outlook, and an honest, pure heart. ... Pulkheria Alexandrovna was sentimental, but not maudlin, she was timid and yielding, but only to a certain point: she could concede a great deal, and consent to much, even with regard to things that went against her convictions, but there was always a limit of honest principle and deep-rooted convictions which nothing could make her overstep. (160)

Like all the characters in *Crime and Punishment*, Pulkheria Alexandrovna is a foil to Raskolnikov, and nowhere is it more explicitly spelled out than in these descriptions. The narrator's positive attitude toward her is felt in almost every word. Although she is forty-three, she looks much younger than her years, having preserved some of her former beauty into old age. Moreover, the narrator attributes her youthful, attractive appearance to her high moral character. He repeats the word "preserve" three times, emphasizing that Pulkheria Alexandrovna still possesses those spiritual qualities that we may assume Raskolnikov once had, but now has lost. Raskolnikov's story, in a way, fits the sentimental pattern of the innocent young provincial who comes to seek his fortune in the capital, where, waylaid by the forces of evil, he succumbs to corruption and loses all traces of his former freshness and purity. Only Raskolnikov succumbs not to the temptations of high society like Balzac's Rastignac or Stendhal's Julien Sorel, but to those of rationalistic Petersburg. In contrast to his mother, Raskolnikov is seriously disturbed in spirit. Essentially delirious through large parts of the novel, he experiences few moments of inner peace. He is a man against himself, for he has almost willfully brought on his own destruction.

Pulkheria Alexandrovna's fresh outlook also contrasts sharply with the lethal and dark theories of her son. Closeted in a room in which a man of average size can hardly stand, breathing in the fetid fumes from the local taverns, hypersensitive and proud, Raskolnikov can hardly escape the adverse effects of his surroundings. He despairs with good reason. His mind is clouded, his living conditions are wretched, and his isolation is almost total.

But the most important quality which the narrator ascribes to Pulkheria Alexandrovna, and which reflects most adversely on Raskolnikov, is her honest and pure heart. Raskolnikov himself confesses to Sonya that his evil heart may have been one of the prime motives for the murder. Although intellectual pride has not completely negated the good impulses of Raskolnikov's heart, it has sufficiently stifled them to enable him to wade through blood without the slightest consciousness of guilt. Only in the epilogue does feeling begin to displace intellect as the guiding force in Raskolnikov's life. The narrator's praise of Pulkheria Alexandrovna's pure heart is more than a negative verbal echo; it transforms Raskolnikov's mother into an implied criticism of her son whenever she is present or spoken of.

Though the second part of the quotation, like the first, is comprised of explicit praise of Pulkheria Alexandrovna, it is more specific and even more cogently bears on Raskolnikov's situation. The narrator commends Pulkheria Alexandrovna for maintaining a limit of honest principle and deep-rooted conviction which nothing could make her overstep. The word used here for "overstep" is *perestupit'*, which in addition can mean "to cross over", "to transgress", or "to commit a crime". (The first part of the novel's title comes from the substantive form of this verb.)[3]

---

[3] For an interesting note on the various meanings of the novel's Russian title (*Prestuplenie i nakazanie*), see J. Thomas Shaw, "Raskol'nikov's Dreams," *Slavic and East European Journal*, 17 (1973), 141.

Whereas in English "overstepping", "crime", and "transgression" all have their own fairly well-defined spheres of meaning, in Russian the same word does service for all three concepts. Dostoevsky's choice of this word is, of course, deliberate. And, as we might expect, he plays upon its various meanings throughout the novel. In the discussion of Raskolnikov's article alone (Part Three, Chapter Five), the word and its synonyms and derivatives occur seventeen times. Moreover, verbal echoes abound. We even find Luzhin telling Dunya that there is in all things a limit beyond which it is dangerous to cross. Like several other key concepts and words, *perestupit'* constitutes part of a finely wrought system of reverberations. Dostoevsky is not simply a creator of fascinating characters, he is also an artist of the word.

Although Pulkheria Alexandrovna may on occasion consent to that which goes against her convictions, she maintains a core of inviolable principles. Raskolnikov, on the other hand, not only transgresses the laws of nature, man, and God, he casuistically uses his convictions to justify his crimes. He believes that he can exploit, even dispose of, people to advance his own ends. His rare statements that he killed for others cannot be taken seriously. Indeed, he confesses several times to Sonya that he murdered for himself alone, and not for others, not for his mother, not for his sister, and certainly not for humanity: "... at that time I couldn't have cared less if I spent my life like a spider catching men in my web and sucking out their life juices!" (324) And although Raskolnikov mentions once or twice that he would have atoned a hundredfold for his crime by devoting the rest of his life to humanity, and that he murdered solely to procure the means by which to accomplish his mission, not once does he tell us about his humanitarian plans for the future. The reason for this reticence I believe is quite clear: Raskolnikov simply has no such plans, and given his character, it is difficult to imagine him having any. He despises not only the socialists, but human beings in general. He dreams not of helping his fellowman, but of exploiting him, killing with impunity to demonstrate that he has the makings of a great benefactor. In his twisted logic, great murderers become great benefactors.

In fact, again in direct contrast to his mother, Raskolnikov has no unshakable, inviolable convictions; for they, of course, are impossible without stalwart principles. Throughout the novel Raskolnikov alternately abandons and adopts new positions. He no sooner tries to help a young girl who has just been seduced, than he concludes that his efforts are useless in view of the social law, according to which a certain percentage of young girls must be sacrificed for the good of all. He gives

Katerina Ivanovna money only to regret his action moments later. Indeed, the only convictions that he maintains through most of the novel proper are that he is better than others and that the murder of the pawnbroker was no crime. But even these convictions are shaken by his growing awareness that he has failed to execute the murder according to plan, and thus that he belongs to the category of ordinary beings for whom murder is a crime.

In contrast to her son, Pulkheria Alexandrovna possesses the integration necessary for maintaining strong principles, and a basic honesty that prevents her from abandoning them for expediency. The narrator's praise of Pulkheria Alexandrovna then is a thinly disguised indirect attack both on Raskolnikov's abandonment of those honest principles that are the truest definition of his mother's moral being and on his consequent entry into a universe where transgression becomes not only possible, but inevitable.

This positive commentary is especially significant in light of recent criticism questioning the purity of Pulkheria Alexandrovna's motives. Snodgrass, for example, views her as one of the novel's minor villains, arguing that because she consciously aggravates Raskolnikov's feelings of guilt for his family's indigent condition, she must bear partial responsibility for his murder of the pawnbroker.[4] It is tempting to read all sorts of things into Pulkheria Alexandrovna's relationship with Raskolnikov. Depending on how one interprets her letter to her son, one might condemn her for consenting to the sacrifice of Dunya or for playing insidiously on Raskolnikov's guilt feelings to stir him to action. But though the notebooks show a good deal of antagonism between mother and son, and though the facts, it must be admitted, cut both ways, one cannot make Raskolnikov's mother into a minor villain without completely disregarding the narrator's explicit commentary. For it does not seem likely that the spokesman for the implied author would ascribe high and honest principles to a mother who willingly sacrifices her own daughter or deliberately exploits her son's feelings of guilt.

On the contrary, it seems that the commentary here is designed to resolve much of the ambiguity that can be read into Pulkheria Alexandrovna's relationship with Raskolnikov. Though this perhaps makes her

---

[4] W. D. Snodgrass, "Crime for Punishment: The Tenor of Part One," *Hudson Review*, 13 (1960), 215–21, 234–40, 251, 252. Edward Wasiolek in *Fyodor Dostoevsky, The Notebooks for "Crime and Punishment,"* trans. and ed. by Edward Wasiolek (Chicago: Univ. of Chicago Press, 1967), pp. 11–13, also sees Raskolnikov's mother in a negative light, alshough he does not go nearly so far as Snodgrass in blaming her for Raskolnikov's situation.

less interesting as a character in her own right, it makes her a better foil to her son. And, in fact, it is the values represented by his mother that Raskolnikov comes back to in the end. In the wide expanses of Siberia, far away from the intellectual and physical poisons of the capital, Raskolnikov experiences a purification of the heart and a rebirth of the spirit.[5]

Any analysis of extended commentary in *Crime and Punishment* would be deficient without examining the narrator's explicitly stated opinions on Razumikhin. Most of them occur in a lengthy passage at the end of Part One, Chapter Four, preceding Razumikhin's first appearance.

But with Razumikhin, for some reason, he [Raskolnikov] made friends, that is, he didn't exactly make friends, but was more open and communicative with him. With Razumikhin, however, it was impossible to be on any other terms. He was an uncommonly cheerful and communicative fellow, so good-hearted that he seemed simple. But concealed beneath this simplicity were both depth and dignity. The better among his friends understood this and loved him. He was quite intelligent, though sometimes he really was somewhat naive. His appearance was striking — he was tall and thin with black hair, and was always badly shaved. Sometimes he could make a row, and he was reputed to possess exceptional strength. One night, in the company of some friends, he knocked down an enormous policeman with one blow. He had an unlimited capacity for drink, but he could completely abstain; sometimes he would play rather unpleasant tricks, but he could do without this too. Razumikhin was especially remarkable in that no failure could discourage him, and no adverse circumstances, it seemed, could crush him. He could live even on the roof, tolerate extreme hunger and extraordinary cold. He was very poor, but was completely self-supporting, earning money at all sorts of odd jobs. He knew virtually hundreds of ways of earning money. Once he didn't heat his room for a whole winter and maintained that it was even more pleasant that way because one sleeps better in the cold. At present, he also had been compelled to leave the university, but only for a short time, and he was trying to do all in his power to straighten his affairs, so that he could continue his studies. (44–5)

The narrator's praise of Razumikhin is evident from the very first sentence, and it continues unabated to the end of the passage. There

---

[5] For a positive evaluation of Pulkheria Alexandrovna, see Richard Curle, *Characters of Dostoevsky: Studies from Four Novels* (London: Heinemann, 1950), pp. 49–56.

seem to be few virtues which Razumikhin lacks. He is so good-hearted
that he appears simple, but beneath his simplicity we are told are
concealed considerable depth and a sense of dignity. Furthermore, he is
quite intelligent. Even Razumikhin's foibles turn out to be virtues in
disguise. His tendency to be rambunctious, his capacity for drink, his
mischievous behavior — all of which he can control when the occasion
demands — are but indications of his tremendous vitality. In addition,
they make him more endearing and human.

The primary function of this encomium, like the one to Pulkheria
Alexandrovna, is to shed light on Raskolnikov. By placing the narrator's
detailed comments considerably earlier than Razumikhin's first appearance, Dostoevsky makes the reader conscious from the beginning of those
areas in which Razumikhin and Raskolnikov are to be compared and
contrasted. Yet by novel's end, the reader does not feel the commentary
either obtrusive or unwarranted, since it is so often corroborated by
Razumikhin's thoughts and actions. Though this praise is strongly
worded and in places quite explicit, it cannot stand alone; it cannot by
itself make Razumikhin a believable foil to Raskolnikov. Dostoevsky
must give solid evidence to back it up; he must substantiate his narrator's praise by facts. In this way, commentary and action are woven
into a tightly knit web. Whereas the action establishes the soundness of
commentary; commentary foreshadows the action and provides the
reader with an evaluative framework by which to judge it.

Every word of the description of Razumikhin bears on Raskolnikov's
situation. The narrator states that Razumikhin is cheerful and easy
to get along with, traits that by their presence or absence, Dostoevsky
uses to evaluate not only Raskolnikov but other characters as well.
Razumikhin is on good terms with Porfiry, Zosimov, Pulkheria Alexandrovna, and even Raskolnikov's landlady and her servant girl Nastasya.
The only ones who find him a nuisance or sincerely dislike him are
Raskolnikov, Svidrigaylov, and Luzhin. The fact that Raskolnikov could
not really make friends with Razumikhin is not a point in his favor: it
shows the extent of his inability to relate to other human beings.

The narrator's praise of Razumikhin's intelligence is also significant.
Though he may appear a simpleton (to Raskolnikov and Luzhin, for
example), he is presented throughout the novel as the personification of
the healthy intellect, the epitome of right reason — thus living up to his
name, which in Russian means intelligence. Razumikhin is not Raskolnikov's intellectual inferior, and the narrator's commentary assures the
reader that this is so.

Though modesty leads him to disparage his talent, Razumikhin knows German well enough to translate difficult texts for publication. (It is implied that Raskolnikov does not.) Like Fetyukovich, Dmitry's lawyer in *The Brothers Karamazov* — but at the same time, without being the object of the narrator's biting irony — Razumikhin brilliantly reconstructs the events of the crime and correctly assesses the character and psychology of the murderer. He is thoroughly conversant with all the burning theoretical questions of the day and acutely conscious of the absence of original thinking among the members of his own generation. Yet he derives great pleasure from actively debating the issues with his friends. He immediately recognizes the secondhand quality of Luzhin's ideas of enlightened self-interest and quickly cuts through to the core of Raskolnikov's argument on crime, thus elucidating the major cause of the murder as accurately as he had reconstructed the details of the crime and the psychology of the criminal.

But in alluding to Razumikhin's depth and intelligence, the narrator obviously has in mind something broader and more important than mental acumen. Razumikhin possesses those aspects of the human intelligence essential for living a productive life in trying circumstances. To be sure, Razumikhin uses his wits to survive, translating tedious scientific texts and finding work where little is to be found, but his greatest gift rests in understanding the difference between sterile theory and the living soul. Razumikhin in short has a greater understanding of real life than Raskolnikov, whose rationalism leads not to life's affirmation but to its destruction. Therein lies the depth of which the narrator speaks in his encomium.

The narrator's positive commentary in the above passage and its later confirmation in the novel also effectively underscore the opposite response of Raskolnikov and Razumikhin to nearly identical material situations. Razumikhin, like Raskolnikov, is an impoverished law student, but he is even worse off. His furniture and clothes are in poorer condition. Indeed his poverty was so great one winter, the narrator tells us, that he was unable to heat his room.

Raskolnikov is crushed physically and psychologically by his poverty. He receives money from his mother and sister; but it is of no help, for he refuses out of spite and pride to supplement it by work. He makes no effort to return to the university (his books are thickly coated with dust); rather he lies in his room and dreams of forging his career with the blow of an ax.

Razumikhin, by contrast, is completely self-supporting. We learn later that he has a rich uncle, but on principle refuses a loan. He even seems to thrive on poverty, enduring hunger, cold, and privation in good spirits. His excellent humor is amply demonstrated throughout the novel. Although compelled by circumstances to leave the university, he is actively engaged in all sorts of jobs so that he can reenter as soon as possible. He is willing to work hard to make his career. He has concrete plans for the future, and in the epilogue he is actually attending classes again. Murder is obviously not the only way out of poverty. Even under extreme conditions, personality plays a far more important role than environment.

The narrator has set up a comparison with Raskolnikov which permits him to comment at the most profound levels on the problems of his hero. Every important trait in the description of Razumikhin is used in this way. Every word of explicit praise resounds through the novel as a standard against which Raskolnikov may be judged. This, in large part, explains the function of extended commentary — why it is invariably so strong and explicit: it firmly establishes a character's personality on his first appearance so that he may serve from then on as a clearly defined foil.

It becomes clear, then, why Dostoevsky uses extended commentary for Razumikhin and various other characters but never for Raskolnikov. He avoids it for the same reason that he avoids any strong and explicit commentary on his hero. Raskolnikov must not be presented in straightforward terms if the novel is to retain its dramatic interest and impact.

Strong commentary, especially when extended and explicit, unquestionably makes the presentation of characters much less suspenseful. Dostoevsky's different method of dramatizing Razumikhin and Raskolnikov demonstrates this point quite clearly. Only one extended passage of narrational commentary deals with Razumikhin, yet it is so explicit that it effectively determines how the reader perceives him throughout the novel. We expect him to act in a certain way, and he fulfills our expectations. He is, to be sure, handled dramatically in that after he is introduced he is presented only through his own thoughts, words, and actions; but it is a static type of dramatization: it merely illustrates what the narrator has already said.

The dramatization of Raskolnikov is handled in a different way, and consequently produces a significantly different effect. Although the narrator often uses commentary with Raskolnikov, it is usually subtle. Since, with the exception of the epilogue, it is never explicit, it does not offer a neat and definitive explanation of Raskolnikov's behavior. Whereas all Razumikhin's actions are predictable and merely confirm the narrator's analysis, every action of Raskolnikov seems to introduce a new facet of his personality and thus his character appears to be slowly revealed throughout the entire novel. The final answer to Raskolnikov's identity is given, if at all, only in the epilogue. The presentation of Raskolnikov is thus dramatic in a higher sense: it depends not only on a predominance of showing over telling, but on a specific relationship between the two. Both Razumikhin and Raskolnikov are for the most part characterized through action, thought, and conversation, but with Raskolnikov the very process by which we come to know him has been effectively dramatized.

The critics who have noted the presence of strong narrational commentary in *Crime and Punishment*, especially the extended type, have argued that Dostoevsky employs it only for secondary characters, because there is no need for them to be presented as objectively and dramatically as Raskolnikov.[6] These critics seem to be implying that Dostoevsky's subtle treatment of Raskolnikov was a conscious departure from tradition, whereas his handling of secondary characters was merely a mechanical adherence to established forms. Since they interpret strongly worded commentary as an artistic deficiency rather than a valuable novelistic device with specific, often crucial, functions, it is not hard to understand why they have failed to give this type of commentary the attention it deserves.

The most obvious explanation for the differences in technique with various characters is economy. Having a figure reveal himself merely through action, thought, and conversation, or occasionally exposing him through flashes of brief and subtle commentary is an effective but time-consuming process. Such a method, though necessary for the hero and perhaps a few other important characters, would certainly prove tedious and ineffective for relatively minor characters. So, whereas Svidrigaylov and Raskolnikov, who appear in more scenes and receive greater attention than any other characters, are handled with circumspection by the narrator, many of the other characters — Luzhin, Pulkheria Alexandrovna, Razumikhin, Katerina Ivanovna — are subjected to rather strong and often explicit commentary. But economy alone cannot explain the

---

6 Johannes van der Eng, *Dostoevskij romancier: Rapports entre sa vision du monde et ses procédés littéraires* (The Hague: Mouton, 1957), p. 70; F. I. Evnin, "Roman 'Prestuplenie i nakazanie,'" *Izvestija Akademii nauk*, 24, No. 1 (1965), 77–8.

ways in which the narrator reveals his characters. Such secondary personages as Porfiry Petrovich and Marmeladov receive almost no narrational
commentary. And others who are the subject of strong and even extended
commentary, in many scenes are treated as objectively and dramatically as
Raskolnikov himself: once the narrator has let us know his feelings about
a character, especially in an extended analysis, he rarely needs to use
further commentary; the reader can interpret all the character's subsequent actions in light of the narrator's initial assessment. Razumikhin's
involvement in Raskolnikov's life, for example, is presented almost
entirely through action and dialogue; and this is as true for his nursing of
Raskolnikov as for his courting of Dunya. In fact, as we have seen, the
narrator even takes time to dramatize Razumikhin's inner life. With
Razumikhin, extended commentary does not exclude dramatization.

The same combination of drama and commentary is also used for
other important figures. Even Luzhin is to a large extent presented
dramatically. Except for several lengthy passages in which the narrator
takes some brief but merciless jabs at Luzhin's motives and ethical
standards, Luzhin's role is an active one. He is the focal point of three of
the novel's most dramatic scenes, which, in addition to being parallel in
structure, are made up almost exclusively of dialogue. In each scene,
Luzhin takes the offensive. His visit to Raskolnikov's apartment, his
falling-out with Dunya and Pulkheria Alexandrovna, and his exposure
at Marmeladov's funeral feast are almost identical in structure. At Raskolnikov's he attempts to show off his intelligence and his newly acquired
progressive views, and at both the family gathering and at Marmeladov's
funeral feast, he attempts to discredit Raskolnikov before Dunya and her
mother by defaming Sonya. In every case, threatened with bodily harm,
Luzhin beats a hasty and humiliating retreat: Raskolnikov threatens to
throw him down the stairs; Razumikhin to break his head; and the
drunken crowd at the funeral feast to turn him over to the police. The
treatment of Luzhin, like the presentation of Razumikhin, shows that
strongly worded commentary and dramatization are not mutually
exclusive. No really significant correlation exists between the use of this
commentary in evaluating a character and the extent to which he is
presented dramatically. In fact no generalizations can be made about the
techniques of narrational commentary used with the various characters
beyond that they perform specific and crucial functions in the novel.

Though the narrator's commentary does not adhere to any simple rule
of thumb, it is never employed arbitrarily. The treatment of some characters is necessitated by economy — to keep the focus on the action and

the hero. The treatment of others is determined by the need to make explicit contrasts with Raskolnikov. And the exclusion of Raskolnikov from any extended and explicit commentary sets him apart and makes the commentary that occurs at the end of the epilogue all the more forceful for being unique.

CHAPTER 8

PHYSICAL DESCRIPTION OF
THE CHARACTERS

Another tool of the narrator in *Crime and Punishment* that has not been sufficiently studied is physical description.[1] Since this technique invites the reader to infer a character's moral worth on the basis of his appearance, it is almost never explicit, though it may be, as in Lebezyatnikov's case, rather heavy-handed. The physical description, like all other devices of narrational commentary, guides the reader's judgment and colors his perception of characters and events. It is, however, particularly effective in bringing the narrator's point of view to bear on characters for whom there is no other commentary.

In general Dostoevsky's handling of physical descriptions conforms to nineteenth-century practice: he incorporates most of them into the introductory passages accompanying the character's first appearance. After the initial description, the narrator provides few additional details. Dostoevsky's technique in *Crime and Punishment* is quite different from that of the early Tolstoy, who uses physical detail as leitmotifs, repeating a character's most outstanding traits each time he appears. In Tolstoy, as Merezhkovsky has shown, physical details take on spiritual and moral qualities.[2] Each crack of Aleksey Karenin's knuckles, each flash of Anna Karenina's fathomless grey eyes reveals in its own way as much about

---

[1] A. A. Belkin, *Čitaja Dostoevskogo i Čexova: Stat'i i razbory* (M.: Xudožestvennaja literatura, 1973), pp. 78–80, notes that physical descriptions are to a certain degree ideological in that "Dostoevsky attempts to reveal the idea of the person in the description of his face." (p. 80) He does not pursue this observation, however. The only study that I have come across devoted to the physical descriptions in a specific novel by Dostoevsky is that of I. V. Ètov, in "Manera povestvovanija v romane Dostoevskogo 'Idiot,'" *Vestnik Moskovskogo universiteta*, 21, No. 1 (1966), 70–6. Ètov, no more than Belkin, discusses how the descriptions are incorporated in the evaluative structure of the novel.

[2] D. S. Merežkovskij, *L. Tolstoj i Dostoevskij: Žizn', tvorčestvo i religija* in *Polnoe sobranie sočinenij*, 7 (St. P.: M. O. Vol'f, 1912), pp. 145–67.

their inner being as their words and deeds. Our dislike of Karenin and attachment to Anna owe as much to what they look like as to what they do.

Though Dostoevsky puts less stress on physical appearance than does Tolstoy, and rarely resorts to Tolstoy's technique of using traits as leit-motifs, he nevertheless uses physical description in *Crime and Punishment* to reveal the inner reality of his characters. His technique differs from Tolstoy's, but his purpose is the same.

Dostoevsky's physical descriptions are far from uniform. Some are almost totally divorced from the action, whereas others are subtly incorporated into the perception of one or more of the characters. The narrator literally stops the action to give his description of Lebezyatnikov, whereas Alyona Ivanovna, the pawnbroker, is presented almost totally from Raskolnikov's point of view. Thus an understanding of the full range and use of the evaluative physical description in *Crime and Punishment* requires examining the descriptions of several minor and major characters.

The character whose physical appearance is least described in *Crime and Punishment* is Raskolnikov. Little is learned about how he looks from the perceptions and remarks of other characters. A prostitute calls him good-looking, after he first pays her a compliment. But another prostitute notes how thin he is and asks him if he has just been released from the hospital. On seeing him when she arrives in Petersburg, Pulkheria Alexandrovna thinks he is better looking than Dunya, but this could easily be interpreted as a mother's prejudice in favor of her first-born. The narrator's remark in Part Three that, facially, Dunya resembles Raskolnikov also gives little concrete information. In fact, the only concrete description of Raskolnikov in the entire novel is but one sentence long. It occurs towards the beginning of the first chapter and is presented from the narrator's perspective. "He was, by the way, remark-ably good-looking, with beautiful dark eyes, brown hair, taller than average, slender, and well-built." (8) The narrator's description is essen-tially factual and neutral. It is true that it establishes that Raskolnikov is, in fact, good-looking, but good looks in *Crime and Punishment* are not a necessarily positive attribute: Luzhin and Svidrigaylov are young-looking, well dressed, and attractive. The word "beautiful", used to describe Raskolnikov's eyes, is the only adjective that might be inter-preted as evaluative. Perhaps Dostoevsky, who often uses the eyes as a symbolic mirror of the soul, is pointing out Raskolnikov's potential for good. Yet the description may just as easily be interpreted as fact.

The brevity of the description, however, is also significant. There are several good reasons why it had to be so short. A lengthy portrait of the hero so early in the novel would certainly have seriously damaged the drama of Raskolnikov's story and the enigma of his personality. The description could not have been presented from the perspective of a character (a much more subtle way of handling this matter) because in the first two parts of the novel Raskolnikov is the only figure whose perception is reported. Since the descriptions presented from the narrator's point of view are much less open to question than that of the characters, Dostoevsky had to keep his narrator's remarks short and as nonevaluative as possible. In addition, by giving so little information about Raskolnikov's physical appearance Dostoevsky further confines the drama of *Crime and Punishment* to the mind and soul of the hero, to an exploration of the spirit, not the flesh.

At the other extreme is the physical description of Lebezyatnikov, the most indisputably negative in the novel. Since it has been analyzed from a slightly different angle in the previous chapter, I shall quote only the sections relevant to my present purpose.

> This Andrey Semenovich was a cachectic, scrofulous, short fellow who served in some ministry. He had peculiarly flaxen hair and sported muttonchop whiskers of which he was very proud. Moreover, he constantly had trouble with his eyes. He was kindhearted enough, but his particularly self-assured speech always turned out to be ridiculously incongruous with his small size. (282)

The description differs little from the strongest narrational commentary. In fact, at first glance, it seems more censure than description. The modifiers "cachectic" and "scrofulous" set the whole tone. It is doubtful that Lebezyatnikov is actually suffering from either cachexia or scrofula; but his poor eyesight and peculiarly flaxen hair suggest that he is an albino, and this alone would certainly explain his anemic and emaciated appearance.[3] In any case, the narrator could hardly have chosen more evaluative diseases. Both are chronic illnesses involving physical deterioration and rather striking symptoms: glandular swelling in scrofula and emaciation in cachexia. And the narrator is obviously equating Lebezyatnikov's sickly constitution with his half-baked radical ideas. Like his physical symptoms, Lebezyatnikov's convictions are concrete evidence of

---

[3] Belkin, p. 78, notes that the eyes "in all Dostoevsky's portraits are the most important and meaningful part of the face. Through them one can penetrate ... into the person's soul."

a fundamentally unsound organism. They are the product of an unhealthy intellect. Lebezyatnikov thus attests Dostoevsky's ability to create a type, much as Gogol does, out of an exaggerated physical description. The implication is unmistakable: a direct relationship exists between the mental and physical; physical reality is but the external image of the spirit within.

The physical description of Lebezyatnikov, however, is not completely static, for his poor eyesight plays as important a role as his good heart in Luzhin's exposure at Marmeladov's funeral feast. One will remember that Lebezyatnikov is present when Luzhin slips a hundred-ruble note into Sonya's pocket in order to further stain her already tarnished reputation. Luzhin knows that Lebezyatnikov is nearsighted and therefore believes he can perform the operation undetected. Luzhin's plan, however, miscarries: Lebezyatnikov sees him and later speaks out against him. Luzhin counters, pointing out that Lebezyatnikov, with his poor eyesight, could never have seen the note all the way from the window. But Lebezyatnikov will not be denied: "No, I didn't imagine it. And though I was standing far away I saw everything. It was really difficult to make out the note — you're right about that — but I happened to know for sure that it was precisely the hundred-ruble note, because when you were giving Sonya Semenovna the ten-ruble note — I saw it all — you then took a hundred-ruble note from the table (I saw this, because I was standing quite close then; and because a certain thought instantly came to my mind, I did not forget that you had the note in your hands) ... and I finally saw you succeed in slipping the note into her pocket." (308–9) By corroborating one detail of the narrator's earlier description of Lebezyatnikov, his poor eyesight, this episode lends credibility to all the other details of Lebezyatnikov's appearance regardless of how little further support they receive in the text. Although the description of Lebezyatnikov is the most heavy-handed one in the novel, Dostoevsky manages to give it validity by subtly verifying it in one of the most dramatic scenes.

With Lebezyatnikov we further see how physical traits can take on moral implications. We understand Lebezyatnikov's physical disability in a figurative sense, and, what is more, using associative logic we interpret his illness to be a criticism, not solely of Lebezyatnikov, but of a whole generation of like-thinking progressives. Physical description has been transformed into indirect evaluative commentary.

The portrayal of Lebezyatnikov is atypical in that no other physical description in *Crime and Punishment* even approaches its lavish use of invective. In the manner in which it is presented, however, it resembles other descriptions that are strictly from the narrator's point of view by being straightforward, strongly worded, and set off from the surrounding text. This is as true for the portraits of Razumikhin, Dunya, and Pulkheria Alexandrovna as it is for that of Lebezyatnikov. Since I have already discussed Pulkheria Alexandrovna and Razumikhin in some detail, I shall focus here on the description of Dunya:

> Razumikhin, of course, was ridiculous in his sudden, drink-inflamed passion for Avdotya Romanovna; but looking at Avdotya Romanovna, especially now when she was pacing the room, arms folded, sad and pensive, many would have excused him, apart from his unusual condition. Avdotya Romanovna was remarkably good-looking, tall, strikingly svelte, strong, and self-confident — the last was evident in her every gesture and by no means took away from the softness and grace of her movements. In face she resembled her brother, but one might have called her a beauty. She had light brown hair, somewhat lighter than her brother's; her almost black, flashing eyes were proud, but they could also be extraordinarily kind. She had a pale complexion, but it was a healthy pallor; her face shone with freshness and health. Her mouth was a little small, and her lower lip, vibrant and scarlet, along with her chin, protruded ever so slightly — this was the only irregularity in this beautiful face, but at the same time, it gave it a special character and a certain haughtiness. Her expression was always more serious and pensive than gay; on the other hand, how well her smile suited her face, how well her gay, young, and wholehearted laughter became her! It is understandable that Razumikhin, ardent, open, jovial, honest, fabulously strong, and intoxicated, who moreover had seen nothing comparable to Dunya, would lose his head at first sight. Besides, as if fated, he saw Dunya for the first time at a moment when love and joy at seeing her brother made her especially beautiful. He later saw her lower lip tremble with indignation in response to her brother's arrogant and cruel commands — and he could not resist. (159–60)

This description is particularly important because it is the only place in the novel that the narrator outspokenly expresses his attitude toward Dunya. The description glows with admiration: "Razumikhin, of course, was ridiculous in his ... passion for Avdotya Romanovna; but looking at Avdotya Romanovna, especially now ... many would have excused him." She is tall, svelte, and remarkably good-looking; her eyes are kind, and her smile gay, young, and wholehearted; her face shines with freshness and health. Although "kind" is perhaps the only explicitly evaluative word in the passage, the other physical expressions for physical beauty, especially in the context of the narrator's commendatory tone, all take on spiritual qualities. Her flashing eyes reveal a vibrant and healthy spiritual life, just as the glow in her cheeks speaks of physical well-being.

Although Dunya looks remarkably like her brother, her radiant health contrasts dramatically with Raskolnikov's feverish despair. Indeed, the reader can only interpret the narrator's admiration for Dunya as indirect, but nevertheless strong, criticism of Raskolnikov's physical and spiritual condition. Since the similarity of brother and sister in appearance, as well as temperament, is stressed throughout, every word in praise of Dunya's freshness and radiant health underlines Raskolnikov's prostration and despondency. Raskolnikov lacks his sister's healthful vigor, not because he lives in Petersburg, although this must not be discounted altogether, but because he has lost all semblance of hope and inner peace.

Though the physical description of Dunya, like most introductory descriptions in *Crime and Punishment*, breaks into the narrative, it is much more smoothly integrated into the text than that of Lebezyatnikov, for it is much less strident and exaggerated. It steers away from hyperbole by introducing slightly negative traits: Dunya's eyes are somewhat proud, her lower lip protrudes, and her face is more serious than gay. Each of these negative characteristics is, of course, more than compensated for by corresponding virtues. Nevertheless a balance is achieved. Furthermore, Dostoevsky uses the description in the narrative by making it explanatory as well as introductory, and by alternating the point of view between the narrator and Razumikhin.

The narrator's role in the description is particularly interesting. Dunya and her mother have been escorted by Razumikhin to their lodgings. They have just experienced an unexpectedly disturbing reunion with Raskolnikov, who fainted on first seeing them and later treated them with open hostility. Before leaving them, Razumikhin tries to allay their fears about Raskolnikov, promising to report promptly on his condition, even swearing that he will have the doctor make a special visit. Anxiously awaiting Razumikhin's promised report, Dunya begins to pace back and forth in her room just as she had on the night she decided to accept Luzhin's proposal of marriage. The narrator does not stop the action, beg the reader's pardon, and launch into a detailed description of Dunya. On the contrary, he seems to transform himself into one of Dunya's admirers, who like Razumikhin finds himself irresistibly carried away by her beauty. Moreover, the description seems motivated, not by the narrator's need to detail the appearance of one more character in the novel, but by his impulse to express admiration for this girl who has become remarkably beautiful at a moment of great inner turmoil. It seems to issue forth naturally, even spontaneously; it is as if the narrator has descended from the Olympian heights of omniscience into the world of his characters. "Her expression was always more serious and pensive than gay; on the other hand, how well her smile suited her face, how well her gay, young, and wholehearted laughter became her!"

The description of Dunya serves a further purpose in that it explains Razumikhin's rather unusual behavior. It is certainly not normal for him (even when drunk) to throw himself down on the pavement begging to kiss the hands of strange women or give them lectures on the younger generation's lack of originality. The reader is shown that he was simply overwhelmed by Dunya's beauty, for as the description comes to a close, it gradually shifts to Razumikhin's point of view. "It is understandable that Razumikhin, ardent, open, jovial, honest, fabulously strong, and intoxicated, who moreover had seen nothing comparable to Dunya, would lose his head at first sight. Besides, as if fated, he saw Dunya for the first time at a moment when love and joy at seeing her brother made her especially beautiful. He later saw her lower lip tremble with indignation in response to her brother's arrogant and cruel commands — and he could not resist."

The description then is triply effective. It provides physical and psychological information about Dunya, an explanation of Razumikhin's strange behavior, and, of course, a set of standards by which Raskolnikov can be effectively characterized and judged.

Although striking, the physical descriptions clearly attributable to the narrator are utilized far less often than those presented from the points of view of the characters themselves. Though the narrator may seem to be merely transcribing perception he often injects into these descriptions significant amounts of commentary. Katerina Ivanovna, Svidrigaylov, Marmeladov, Sonya, Luzhin, Porfiry Petrovich, Alyona Ivanovna and most of the lesser figures in the novel are in varying degrees introduced in this way. An analysis of the descriptions of Zosimov and Svidrigaylov will demonstrate this technique and its significance.

The narrator's introduction of Zosimov, the young doctor helping Razumikhin take care of Raskolnikov, shows a combination of commentary and description from another character's point of view.

"Zosimov! At last!" cried Razumikhin, overjoyed.

Chapter IV

Zosimov was a tall, fat man with a puffy, colorless, smooth-shaven face, and straight flaxen hair; he wore glasses and had a large gold ring on one of his fat-swollen fingers. He was about twenty-seven. He was wearing a loose, stylish summer coat, and light-colored summer trousers, and in general everything he wore was loose, fashionable, and spic and span: his linen was irreproachable and his watch chain enormous. His manner was slow, languorous as it were, but yet studiously free and easy; his pretentiousness, however strenuously he tried to conceal it, continually showed through. Everyone who knew him found him tedious, but said that he knew his business. (104)

The technique employed here certainly resembles narrated perception. Razumikhin and Raskolnikov both have their eyes on Zosimov as he walks in. The description follows directly without an introductory verb of perception: "'Zosimov! At last!' cried Razumikhin, overjoyed. Zosimov was a tall, fat man." For several reasons the perception seems to be Raskolnikov's rather than Razumikhin's. First, the narrator has transcribed up to this point only Raskolnikov's perception. Second, Razumikhin already knows Zosimov quite well and would not be examining him so thoroughly as Raskolnikov, who is seeing him clearly for the first time. (Raskolnikov has been either delirious or unconscious during Zosimov's previous visits.) Third, the unflattering nature of the description appears to reflect Raskolnikov's irritability.

Yet it can also be argued that the passage is basically presented from the narrator's perspective. We can, for example, translate the phrase *Bylo emu let dvadcat' sem'* as "He was about twenty-seven" or "he appeared to be about twenty-seven" depending on whether we think that it represents the narrator's or Raskolnikov's point of view. The last sentence, however, is certainly the narrator's; it is not a physical description at all, but a fact: "Everyone who knew him found him tedious, but said that he knew his business." Furthermore, the chapter division between Zosimov's entrance and the actual description gives the impression that the narrator is beginning a new chapter solely to introduce Zosimov.

Other signs indicate the narrator's presence in the passage as well. Every word, in fact, seems to reveal a consciousness that judges as it describes. Though Zosimov's obesity is a given, we feel that the narrator

is perhaps emphasizing the fact more than would seem necessary. He
calls attention to Zosimov's fat fingers and flabby cheeks, and he seems
intentionally to choose the most unflattering word for fat (*žirnyj*), when
Russian has as many euphemistic and roundabout ways of expressing
this condition as English. The slightly disapproving tone that we sense
throughout the passage becomes particularly noticeable in the narrator's
description of Zosimov's mannerisms. We are told that the foppish young
doctor's free and easy manner is really studiously free and easy, and that
his pretentiousness is continually showing through, despite his efforts to
conceal it. When the narrator says in the last sentence that Zosimov's
acquaintances found him tedious, we feel that this must be the narrator's
opinion as well. In effect, Dostoevsky has it both ways: the description is
simultaneously taken, however unconsciously, to be the narrator's introduction as well as Raskolnikov's perception.

Dostoevsky's handling of the description of Zosimov differs markedly,
however, from that of Dunya and Lebezyatnikov. Whereas the description of Dunya breaks into the narrative, that of Zosimov is incorporated
directly into the action; it is the perception that we assume takes place
immediately after Zosimov enters the room. This is not only a more
scenic way of incorporating description in the narrative but also a more
subtle way of introducing evaluative commentary. Since the description
is on one hand presented as from a character's point of view, the narrator's evaluative remarks are relatively inconspicuous. Yet they nevertheless effectively determine our emotional and moral responses.

Incorporated into Raskolnikov's consciousness to an even greater
extent than the description of Zosimov, is that of Svidrigaylov in Part
Six. There are actually two descriptions of Svidrigaylov in the novel.
The first is a rather neutral description presented strictly from the narrator's point of view. It occurs in Part Three before Svidrigaylov is
formally introduced to the reader.[4] The second occurs rather late in the
novel in a tavern to which Raskolnikov has come in search of Svidrigaylov.

Raskolnikov leaned his right elbow on the table, set his chin in the
fingers of his right hand and stared fixedly at Svidrigaylov. For about
a minute he scrutinized his face, which even before had always struck

---

[4] See *CP*, p. 190. Although the first description is given from the narrator's
point of view, it is rather objective — that is it differs little from what any passerby would have observed on seeing Svidrigaylov at that moment.

him. It was a rather strange face, almost like a mask: white and red, with scarlet lips, a flaxen beard and with still rather thick blond hair. His eyes were somehow too blue, and their expression somehow too heavy and fixed. There was something horribly unpleasant in this handsome face, which, considering its age, was extremely young-looking. Svidrigaylov was wearing fashionable, light, summer clothes, and he had on particularly elegant linen. On his finger was an enormous ring with an expensive stone. (361)

Raskolnikov has for some minutes been attentively listening to Svidrigaylov. Now more than ever, he is resolved to make Svidrigaylov abandon whatever designs he has on Dunya. But he also needs to learn something from Svidrigaylov himself. Svidrigaylov has brought with him a rather romantic, though villainous, reputation from the country. He allegedly has committed three murders, seems to enjoy the best of health, and from all signs is pursuing Dunya as relentlessly as ever. Is he, and not Raskolnikov, the true superman? What are the implications of such an existence? These must be the questions taking shape in Raskolnikov's mind. Moreover, Svidrigaylov is continually bringing up to Raskolnikov how really alike they are. Raskolnikov tries fiercely to deny even the possibility of such a comparison, but his very protest indicates that he cannot dismiss it altogether. It is with more than curiosity, then, that Raskolnikov stares at Svidrigaylov in this passage: he is trying to penetrate into Svidrigaylov's soul.

The passage seems to be a paradigmatic case of narrated perception. Whereas in the description of Zosimov we only assume that it is Raskolnikov who is doing the perceiving, in the above description there seems to be little doubt. Raskolnikov places his chin in his hand to get a better look at Svidrigaylov, and the narrator tells us not only that Raskolnikov stared at Svidrigaylov, but that he examined his face for about a minute, adding that it had already made a deep impression on him. The description follows in the next sentence without a verb of perception: "It was a rather strange face, almost like a mask." It proceeds in this manner until Raskolnikov renews the conversation.

Yet, even in this passage, the presence of the narrator can be felt. It must be conceded that it is a subtle presence; but one need only compare the passage with some of the descriptions from Joyce's *Portrait of the Artist as a Young Man*, for example, to appreciate how much this picture of Svidrigaylov is the narrator's view. Note, for instance, how Joyce prepares and presents Stephen Dedalus' perception of Brother Michael:

Brother Michael was standing at the door of the infirmary and from the door of the dark cabinet on his right came a smell like medicine. That came from the bottles on the shelves. The prefect spoke to Brother Michael and Brother Michael answered and called the prefect sir. He had reddish hair mixed with grey and a queer look. It was queer that he would always be a brother. It was queer too that you could not call him sir because he was a brother and had a different kind of look. Was he not holy enough or why could he not catch up on the others?[5]

This is purely Stephen's perception. It is evident in the vocabulary, the sentence structure, and the nature and sequence of impressions. The uninvolved, short, straightforward sentences clearly reflect the consciousness of a young boy. There is a definite progression from one perception to the other: "... from the door of the dark cabinet on his right came a smell like medicine. That came from the bottles on the shelves." What is more, the sentences are tied together by an associative logic that can only be Stephen's. One need only remark the seemingly illogical way that the words "brother", "look", and "queer" are combined: "He [Brother Michael] had ... a queer look. It was queer that he would always be a brother." Furthermore, the description is everywhere surrounded by narrated speech: the last sentence is a particularly good example: "Was he not holy enough or why could he not catch up on the others?" It is impossible to take the description from anyone's but Stephen's perspective.

In contrast, in the description of Svidrigaylov, there are no signs, except for the introductory verbs of seeing, that indicate we are in Raskolnikov's consciousness. There are no traces of narrated speech, no associative word patterns, and no idiosyncrasies we can associate exclusively with Raskolnikov. And certain elements point to the narrator. The portrait is methodical; it moves quickly, but nevertheless is complete. We get a description not only of Svidrigaylov's face but also of his clothing, even his ring and linen. The narrator's frequent use of indefinite qualifiers also makes us doubt that this is totally Raskolnikov's perception. We may concede a few such qualifiers, but we are wary when we find that Svidrigaylov's face was "rather strange", and "almost like a mask", that his eyes were "somehow too blue", and that his look was "somehow too heavy and fixed". The passage seems at times to be more evaluation than perception.

The statement that there was something horribly unpleasant about Svidrigaylov's handsome face, which, considering his age, was extremely

---

[5] *Portrait of the Artist as a Young Man* (New York: Viking, 1964), pp. 22–3.

young-looking, also seems to be an evaluation made at a distance. The very placing of the qualifying phrase, "considering his age", in the middle of the sentence suggests a carefully weighed description much more than it does a character's immediate impression. We might rather expect a picture from Raskolnikov's point of view to read more in the following vein: "His face was certainly well preserved and handsome, but all the same, how really repulsive it was."

The question as to whose perspective the description is presented from is not an idle one. For on it depends our interpretation of the whole passage, and consequently what we may claim to know about Svidri-gaylov. If the narrator is simply transcribing perception, then the picture we get is a subjective one, which perhaps tells us more about Raskol-nikov than Svidrigaylov. If, however, we can even in part attribute the description to the narrator, this picture of Svidrigaylov becomes as important an evaluation of him as any in the novel.

Dostoevsky's purpose, as in all the previous examples, is to reveal the inner from without. With Svidrigaylov, we see a slight variation of this process. Since his face is likened to a mask, we naturally interpret his physical attractiveness and vitality as spiritual deformity and decay. The very connotation of the mask is negative — one does not hide what is seemly — and therefore every detail of the description becomes suspect and perceived negatively. Svidrigaylov's ruddy complexion, for example, does not impress us as favorably as Dunya's healthy pallor. The scarlet lips suggest Svidrigaylov's lust, and the contrast between the bright reds and flaxen whites of his face suggests something inhuman and repulsive, if not demonic. His thick, flaxen hair is but the outline of a mask. His blue eyes, though undoubtedly striking and probably attractive to the ladies, are too blue; his commanding gaze somehow too heavy and fixed. And almost as if the narrator still thinks that he has not convinced the reader that Svidrigaylov's visage is really unattractive and demonic, he adds that there is something horribly unpleasant in this handsome, young-looking face. As we might expect, Svidrigaylov is well dressed, and his linen is especially fine. But his clothing is but another manifesta-tion of the mask: it is the veil thrown over unrestrained sensuality.

The description of Svidrigaylov is thus much more complex than it appears at first. Literature, after all, is not life, and just as in a medieval or modern painting, literary perspective can be multidimensional and often purposefully equivocal. Looked at from the narrator's point of view, the description is perhaps the strongest commentary on Svidri-gaylov before the evening of his suicide. This, of course, is not to say that this is the only passage in which Svidrigaylov's character is revealed. It is obvious in everything he says and has reputedly done. And yet so much of what he says is said for effect, and so much of what he has reputedly done is unsubstantiated, that Svidrigaylov remains an enigma for the better part of the novel. The narrator's commentary, then, couched in physical description, gives a touch of objective validity to the rumor. What is more, it is likely that Raskolnikov sees the very same thing the narrator does and is as repulsed by what he sees as by what he hears. Does he not intuit at this very moment that Svidrigaylov's path leads to nothingness, to spiritual suicide? The portrait of Svidrigaylov is then not only an evaluation of Svidrigaylov but a scathing condemnation of Raskolnikov's steps along the same path.

Because it is incorporated into narrated perception, the physical description of Svidrigaylov economically and unobtrusively limns and evaluates without unduly disrupting the flow of narrative. It also, to some extent, preserves Svidrigaylov's enigmatic quality, which contributes as much to his success as a character in his own right as it does to his success as a foil to Raskolnikov. The incorporated description, however, works as well for minor characters as it does for major ones. It quickly and effectively evaluates figures such as Zosimov so that the narrator can return to his more pressing concern — the story of his hero.

Physical description is thus one more of the narrator's efficient and dramatic instruments of commentary. It may be strident and obtrusive, as with Lebezyatnikov, or neatly incorporated into the narrative. The difference, however, is one of method, not of purpose; for in each case the characters are effectively exposed. And lurking behind the description of almost every character, whether it be Pulkheria Alexandrovna, Razumikhin, Dunya, or Svidrigaylov, is an implicit criticism of Raskolnikov, which gives the physical description, like all the other devices of commentary in *Crime and Punishment*, its ultimate *raison d'être*.

CHAPTER 9

THE NARRATOR, RASKOLNIKOV,
AND THE EPILOGUE

Much of the most striking narrational commentary in *Crime and Punishment* deals with such characters as Pulkheria Alexandrovna, Luzhin, and Razumikhin. The main purpose of this commentary is, however, not the evaluation of secondary characters, but the evaluation of the hero. Explicit statements — often blunt and cutting — about the other characters are one of the narrator's most effective techniques for revealing his attitude toward Raskolnikov.

Yet there is a great deal of evaluative commentary directed at Raskolnikov. It is less often noticed because it tends to be implicit more often than explicit, subtle rather than obtrusive; and because it is frequently incorporated into the transcription of Raskolnikov's consciousness. I have shown how a slight mimicking or a parenthetical "so it seemed to him" is enough to cast Raskolnikov's thoughts in an ironic light. In fact virtually every long passage of narrated consciousness and every interior analysis is a polemical battle between the narrator and his hero. The battle is clearly an unequal one. Unseen by his opponent and impervious to counterattack, the narrator scores all the points. At novel's end the combined effect of these countless pinpricks weighs as heavily against Raskolnikov as the indirect commentary.

It has been mentioned that Dostoevsky's rare use of strongly worded commentary on Raskolnikov makes the presentation of the hero more dramatic and vivid. A further reason has to do with the way in which Raskolnikov is developed during the course of the work.

It is a critical commonplace that the Russian realistic novel of the nineteenth century emphasizes characterization at the expense of plot.[1]

---

[1] D. S. Mirsky, in *A History of Russian Literature from the Earliest Times to the Death of Dostoevsky* (New York: Knopf, 1927), pp. 218–19, states that "another characteristic that ... is typical of them [the realists] as a school is their

This judgment has obviously less relevance to Dostoevsky than to writers like Goncharov, Tolstoy, and Turgenev, but few would question its applicability to *Crime and Punishment*. Yet it may surprise many Anglo-American readers that the psychological drama of *Crime and Punishment* has almost nothing to do with character development — to some a *sine qua non* of great fiction. In fact, there is no character development in the novel at all. Raskolnikov, of course, undergoes an unquestionable change in the epilogue, but this is much more a miraculous transformation than a psychologically motivated and demonstrated process. Raskolnikov does not gradually mend his ways, he is resurrected from the dead, a transformation that defies the laws of time and causality to which most nineteenth-century novels adhere. He is essentially the same person in captivity as he was before the murder. Though enervated and dispirited, he retains his boundless pride and upholds his rationalistic theories well into the last chapter of the epilogue. The drama of *Crime and Punishment* results not from character development but from the slow novel-long revelation of Raskolnikov's personality. And therein lies the explanation of Dostoevsky's restraint in using strong commentary on Raskolnikov. For it is clear that any attempt by the narrator to categorize too strictly or explain too facilely the essence of his hero would resolve the enigma of Raskolnikov's personality, thereby removing the keystone of the novel's dramatic structure.

Nevertheless, in *Crime and Punishment*, the direct commentary on Raskolnikov — the analyses of the hero's motivations, the ironic asides, descriptive epithets, suggestive reminiscences, and finally the famous rhetorical sections of the epilogue in which the narrator suddenly reverses himself and becomes outspoken — all play a crucial role.[2]

A most striking example of the direct form of commentary is the narrator's account of Raskolnikov's reflections immediately before the murder. This commentary is not nearly so heavy-handed as with Lebezyatnikov, nor so open and frank as in the epilogue. Yet, though it is low-keyed, it is in places unequivocal and remarkably effective in undercutting the hero.

---

relative neglect of narrative construction and narrative interest, and the concentration on extra-narrative interest, on character and introspection. In this respect the Russian novel, especially Tolstoy, was far ahead of the European novel of the times and was outdone by Western novelists only in the later work of Henry James, in that of Proust and of James Joyce."

[2] For the examples of direct narrational commentary on Raskolnikov discussed in previous chapters, see pp. 21–2, 53–4, 57–8, 63–7, 87–8.

But these were all trifles, about which he hadn't even thought, nor was there time to. He was thinking about the main thing, and the trifles he was putting off till he was *convinced about everything*. But that seemed absolutely unrealizable. So at least it seemed to him. He could in no way imagine for example that he would ever stop thinking, get up and simply go there. ... Even his recent *trial run* (that is his visit with the intention of giving the place a final looking over) was only a mere *experiment* and far from a serious one, but something like: "Well, why not go and give it a try and see whether I've just been dreaming!" But he immediately flunked the test, spat, and ran away, furious at himself. And yet, it would seem, all analysis, in the sense of the moral resolution of the question, had been completed: his casuistry had become sharp as a razor, and he finally could no longer find conscious objections in his own mind. But in the last resort he simply did not believe himself and stubbornly, slavishly, gropingly sought objections in all directions, as if someone were forcing him and drawing him to do so. The last day, however, which had arrived so unexpectedly and at a blow decided everything, had acted upon him in an almost entirely mechanical manner. It was as if someone had taken him by the hand and drew him along, irresistibly, blindly, with unnatural power, and without objections. It was as if a piece of his clothing had caught in the wheel of a machine and was beginning to drag him in. (59)

At this point Raskolnikov has not irrevocably committed himself to the murder. Although he has already made several important preparations, such as devising a false pledge and sewing a loop inside his coat for the ax, he still cannot believe that he will overcome his intellectual paralysis and actually do the deed. This passage differs from most sections in which Raskolnikov's thoughts are laid out, in that here everything is being told from the narrator's point of view. In fact, it is as much the narrator's analysis as transcription. There is no sentence in which he does not seriously call into question Raskolnikov's motives or his understanding of the situation.

At the beginning of the paragraph, Raskolnikov dismisses the details of his murder plan as trifles that can be put off until he comes to a definite decision — to kill or not to kill. He can hardly conceive, however, that the time is at hand — that he will commit the murder in a matter of hours, and that these trifles, which he summarily refuses to consider, are fated to play a crucial role in his successful perpetration of the crime. The narrator, gifted with hindsight, knows this very well, of course, and we cannot help sensing the irony in his treatment of Raskolnikov's miscalculations. In some respects, Raskolnikov's murder of Alyona Ivanovna is an absurd and macabre comedy of errors, in which the murderer succeeds despite his blundering. Every calculation he makes is wrong, from expecting to find the ax in the kitchen, to assuming that the pawn-broker's sister will be away during the murder. He is saved from his miscalculations not by his wits, in which he takes such pride, but by the most extraordinary concatenation of circumstances: he finds an ax by chance at the caretaker's; he enters the pawnbroker's house shielded by a cart; he meets no one on his way to her room; he escapes by hiding in an empty apartment, conveniently vacated only minutes before; he walks away unnoticed by those congregating in front of the house; he returns safely home, puts back the ax in its former place, and enters his room without having met a single soul. Ironically, the trifles have taken care of themselves; had he planned more carefully, or blundered less, he could hardly have been so successful. But Raskolnikov is not grateful for his success, since it scathingly reveals to him his ineptitude and insignificance: he has proved to himself that he is merely a parody of his Napoleonic ideal.

The narrator's irony, however, becomes plain only in the fourth sentence. After stating that Raskolnikov could not believe that he was capable of doing the deed, the narrator comments: "So at least it seemed to him." The implication is clear: Raskolnikov is as deceived about his own capabilities as he is wrong about what will happen. The interpolated comment here calling attention to Raskolnikov's glaring lack of self-knowledge clearly reveals the narrator's condescending attitude toward his hero and at the same time provides an ironic introduction to the more important commentary that follows.

The narrator reserves his strongest censure for Raskolnikov's moral justification of the murder. He seems to have doubts only about the doing of the deed, and none at all about its moral implications. Here, as in the fourth sentence of the paragraph, a qualifying phrase "it would seem" reveals the narrator's ironic attitude toward Raskolnikov's moral position. But the phrase may also be a means of creating rhetorical surprise. It is as though the narrator himself is amazed that in Raskolnikov's mind the moral questions are easier to resolve than the practical ones. The use of the word casuistry is especially damning; for the Russian term (*kazuistika*) has all the negative force of its English counterpart: the misapplication of ethical principles to individual cases of conduct or conscience. The narrator's likening of Raskolnikov's casuistry to a razor suggests its potential danger and, at least metaphorically, links Raskolnikov's warped thinking with the murder he is soon to commit.

Having challenged Raskolnikov's rationalizations about the contemplated murder, the narrator begins to explode his hero's Napoleonic pretensions. Even before we see him blundering through the murder, Raskolnikov is presented not as a man shaping events, like the world historical figures with whom he compares himself, but as a passive object manipulated by forces beyond his control. His helplessness and passivity are clearly reflected in the grammatical structure of the sentences. He does not act, but is acted upon. It is not he who decides the course of events, but the day. He is led blindly and irresistibly. Raskolnikov has become not the molder, but the material of history.

The final sentence of the paragraph is a fitting conclusion; for it resolves by a metaphor the narrator's two seemingly contradictory positions: that Raskolnikov is caught up in forces beyond his control; and that he is nevertheless fully responsible for the murder. First, the sentence calls attention, even more strongly than any of the preceding material, to Raskolnikov's passivity. He is like a man whose clothing has become caught in the wheel of a machine. He too will be pulled in; it is inevitable; resistance is vain. But while emphasizing Raskolnikov's passivity in order to explode his delusions of grandeur, the narrator does not make his hero into a helpless victim of events; for the machine in the metaphor is of Raskolnikov's own making and design. It is the casuistry that Raskolnikov has used to justify his plans for murder and that removed all the barriers except for the "mere" mechanical details. Once Raskolnikov had been seduced by the specious arguments of rationalism, the murder became not only possible, but according to the logic of the novel, inevitable. Seen from this perspective, the time, place, and manner of the murder are accidental attributes, whereas Raskolnikov's casuistry is its necessary motivating force. Dostoevsky thus portrays Raskolnikov as a victim, not of forces beyond his control, but of the ideas of his own devising. The impersonal machine is a symbol for the mechanistic and inorganic nature of Raskolnikov's rational intellect. It has usurped the place of its master, turned against him, and used him as a tool to realize its own ends. It is as though he had been taken over by an alien force, just like the people in his dream in the epilogue. Perhaps this is why on his way to the pawnbroker Raskolnikov feels like a man condemned to death, and why he will later confess to Sonya that by killing the old woman, he killed only himself. Though Raskolnikov will try time and again to blame fate for his misfortune, Dostoevsky relentlessly shows that he is a victim only in a very special sense, a victim who has willed murder and thus must bear full responsibility for his own fall.

Although the above commentary is devastating, it is essentially implicit, even low-keyed. The narrator makes very few statements about Raskolnikov that are more obtrusive than these. Never does he resort to the type of invective used in the description of Lebezyatnikov. Furthermore, he rarely stops the narrative to express his views on his hero; instead, he incorporates his remarks into the action, in some cases, taking a position so obviously sane and justified by the circumstances that the lack of commentary probably would have been more conspicuous than its presence. Witness, for example, the way he describes Raskolnikov's condition directly after the murder of Lizaveta, the pawnbroker's half-sister.

> Terror was increasingly gaining control over him, especially after this second completely unexpected murder. He wanted to flee as fast as possible. And if at that moment he had been in a condition to see and judge more correctly, if he could only have understood all the difficulties of his situation, its desperateness, ugliness, and absurdity, and realized how many obstacles, perhaps even crimes, there remained for him to overcome and commit, in order to get away and reach home, then it is very likely that he would have abandoned everything and immediately have given himself up, not from fear for himself, but simply from the horror at and revulsion for what he had done. Revulsion, in particular, was growing within him each minute. Not for anything would he have returned to the trunk, not even to the room. (66)

One cannot agree completely with Pierre Hart, who argues that the narrator inserts commentary at this point to stress the repulsiveness and enormity of Raskolnikov's deed.[3] Certainly, there is enough gore to make such commentary superfluous. To halt the action at such a point to moralize on the obvious seems very uncharacteristic of Dostoevsky's method with Raskolnikov. In this passage Raskolnikov is revolted by the events no less than the narrator. The narrator says that Raskolnikov was incapable at that moment of seeing and judging the situation more accurately — not that he was unaffected by his revolting deed. In fact, he experiences this revulsion on several occasions even before the murder. In fact, it seems to be the main force restraining him from committing the crime. Leaving the pawnbroker's on his trial run, Raskolnikov

---

[3] Pierre R. Hart, "Looking over Raskol'nikov's Shoulder: The Narrator in *Crime and Punishment*," *Criticism*, 13 (1971), 170.

exclaims: "'O, God! How revolting it all is! Can I really, really ... no, it's nonsense, it's absurd!' he added decisively. 'How could such a horrible thing have entered my head? What filth my heart is capable of! But the main thing is that it's filthy, low, revolting, revolting! ...'" (12) And in his nightmare of the cruelly beaten horse Raskolnikov experiences horror in some respects rivaling what he feels at the actual murder. He rises from the dream shouting: "God! ... Will I really, really take up an ax? Will I really strike her on the head, smash her skull ... will I really step in the sticky, warm blood, break open the lock, steal and tremble; hide, all covered with blood ... with the ax ... Lord, is it possible?" (50) This revulsion, of course, continues long after the murder. Thus, since the narrator's feelings are not essentially different from Raskolnikov's own, his commentary on this point does not seem particularly obtrusive.

The function of this passage then must be sought elsewhere. One must concede that it contains commentary; but it is of the type with which we are already familiar: subtly but surely the narrator undermines his hero's exalted self-image. Raskolnikov loses complete control of himself at the most crucial moment. Moreover, his rational faculties, in which he takes so much pride and which he believes will see him successfully through the murder, become totally paralyzed. By effectively repeating all the verbs of judgment and perception, the narrator once again emphasizes Raskolnikov's eclipse of reason during the murder: "... if ... he had been in a condition to see and judge more correctly, ... if he could only have understood all the difficulties ... and realized how many ... crimes there remained for him ... to commit."

But this passage does more than deflate Raskolnikov's pretensions, it functions, paradoxically, as a point of psychic relief. We have been through a ten-page description of the murder and the events leading up to it, constructed with almost unrelieved intensity and carefully cultivated impersonality. Doubtless, this impersonality is essential for dramatizing the events to the greatest possible degree. It is one of the prime reasons Dostoevsky discarded first- for third-person narration. But at the same time, this impersonality contrasts markedly with the tone of previous sections. It seems as though the narrator is as mesmerized as the reader by this most gruesome spectacle, as though he is no longer a medium through which the reader perceives the action, but a spectator like ourselves. The passage is like the outburst of an onlooker who can no longer bear the unremitting horror of the sight and must give vent to his emotions. The narrator has, as it were, usurped in part the role of the reader. And it is precisely because of this that we do not feel the passage particularly obtrusive. In fact, it seems perfectly appropriate; for this is where the narrator has been leading us all along. His commentary merely gives voice to our own judgment and emotions.

Though the narrator's point of view in this passage has much in common with the reader's, there are also several significant differences. I have already mentioned his subtle undermining of Raskolnikov's inflated self-image. In addition, he appears to show compassion for this young man, who he knows has entered upon a course of suffering, of which the murder is but one stage. "If he [Raskolnikov] could only have understood all the difficulties ... he would have abandoned everything and immediately have given himself up." We feel the narrator is telling us that Raskolnikov is doing as much violence to himself as to his victim. Raskolnikov may not feel the slightest twinge of guilt, but he recoils in horror and disgust at the deed; and it is this violence which Raskolnikov perpetrates against himself and the suffering that it prophesies that elicit the narrator's compassion.

Dostoevsky, however, did not confine narrational commentary on Raskolnikov to the experiencing self alone. Had he done so, the work would probably have turned out tidier; but it certainly would have sacrificed some of its richness and complexity. The narrator in *Crime and Punishment* talks not of one Raskolnikov, but of two: the one who experiences the events, and the one who is separated from the murder by time and a new world of experience. The reminiscence statements and the explicit commentary of the epilogue introduce us to a totally different temporal realm; and they change not only our temporal perspective, but our view of Raskolnikov as well.

Throughout the novel proper, we find twenty statements in which the narrator alludes to a time from which the events of the novel are recalled long afterwards. These reminiscence passages vary in length, content, and style: some are short and subtly integrated into the narrative; others are of paragraph length and distinguish clearly between past and present.[4] Though one might at first interpret these statements as vestiges of the old first-person notebook plans, close examination shows that they differ from their counterparts in the notebooks both in form and function.

As I illustrated in Chapter Two, the main focus in the notebooks is on the remembering self; consequently, the time of writing is much more vividly felt than the time of the murder. In the final version, the situation

---

[4] *CP*, pp. 14, 51, 53, 56, 62, 64, 67, 71, 75, 87, 93, 94, 127, 243, 272, 308, 318, 339, 358, 403.

is reversed: the past — the time of the murder — greatly overshadows the time from which Raskolnikov looks back on his experiences, really a nebulous period, which may be a more recent past, the present, or even the future. What is more, the narrators are quite different: in the note-books Raskolnikov tells us what he remembers; in the final version Raskolnikov's recollections are reported by an omniscient narrator. The lesser emphasis in the final version on the remembering Raskolnikov, however, should not lead us to underestimate the importance of the reminiscence passages; for they play a crucial role in the novel's temporal and evaluative structure.

Perhaps the most striking of all the reminiscence passages is the one which begins the last part of the novel. Svidrigaylov has just revealed that he has eavesdropped on Raskolnikov's confession of the murder to Sonya. Events are pressing. It is no wonder that Raskolnikov remembers that he lived through this period as if he had been wrapped in an impenetrable fog. His meeting with Porfiry Petrovich and Svidrigaylov can only have loosened his already tenuous hold on reality.

> A strange time began for Raskolnikov. It was as if a fog had fallen over him and imprisoned him in an inescapable and oppressive soli-tude. *Recalling that time later, after much time had already passed,* he surmised that his consciousness had sometimes clouded over, as it were, and that it had so continued, with some intervals, right up to the final catastrophe. He was positively convinced that he had been mis-taken about many things then, for instance, about the time and duration of certain events. In any case, as *he remembered subsequently* and tried to clarify his *memories* to himself, he learned many things about himself, guided by information received from others. He confused, for example, one event with another; and another event he considered the consequence of an occurrence that existed only in his imagination. At times he was overcome by a painful and tormenting anxiety that was turning into a panic-like fear. But he also *remembered* that there were minutes, hours, and even perhaps days, full of an overwhelming apathy — almost in contrast to his former fear — like the morbid indifference that one sometimes observes in the dying. (339) (Italics mine.)

As the italicized words in this passage indicate, the narrator is insistent on making the reader aware of the remembering Raskolnikov. He uses various forms of the word recall four times, and makes it immediately apparent that the past tense applies not to the time of the events, but to the time when the events are recollected. What is more, he stresses that this recollection takes place not simply after, but "long after" the crime: long enough after, evidently, for Raskolnikov to have become a maturer human being, one who has profited from his experience and gained insight into the ideas that led him so far astray.

The recollecting Raskolnikov, however, is not on the same intellectual plane as the narrator: they are separated by a considerable ironic distance. This distance is clearly illustrated in the following passage from Part One, in which Raskolnikov recalls that in walking through Haymarket Square he had learned that Lizaveta, the pawnbroker's sister, would not be home at seven o'clock the following evening.

> Afterwards, when he recalled this time and everything that happened to him during these days, minute by minute, point by point, detail by detail, he was always superstitiously struck by one circumstance, which, though really not very unusual, later constantly seemed to him to have predetermined his fate. That is, he simply could not understand and explain to himself why though thoroughly exhausted he returned home via the Haymarket Square, which was out of his way, rather than the shortest and most direct route. He only made a little detour, but it was an obvious one and absolutely unnecessary. Of course, dozens of times he returned home, not remembering the streets along which he walked. But why, he would always ask, just why did such an important, such a decisive, and at the same time such an extremely accidental meeting on the Haymarket (through which he had no reason to go) occur precisely at that very hour and moment in his life, precisely when he was in such a mood and in such circumstances, when only that meeting could produce the most decisive and fateful consequences for his entire fate? It was as if right there and then it was intentionally lying in wait for him! (51)

The older Raskolnikov obviously has still not gained a complete understanding of his crime; he still seems to believe that he was not the sole author of his fate. The strange combination of circumstances which was to seal his destiny seems to him to have been pre-ordained. It was as though fate had set a trap for him, as though the whole tragedy was part of some higher plan over which he had no control. This view of his crime as a quirk of fate is one that Raskolnikov maintains well into the epilogue, where we find him feeling ashamed but not guilty: "But he judged himself severely and his hardened conscience could not find any particularly terrible guilt in his past, except perhaps for a simple *blunder*, which could have happened to anyone. He was ashamed precisely because he,

Raskolnikov, perished so blindly, hopelessly, meaninglessly, and stupidly, through some decree of blind fate, and was obliged to humble himself and submit to a 'ridiculous' sentence, if he wanted to find any peace at all." (417–18) Although we assume that the older Raskolnikov views the murder as a crime, rather than a mere blunder, he continues to refuse to take full responsibility for his actions. We can be sure, however, that if everything had worked out according to his expectations, Raskolnikov would have vehemently opposed any suggestion that fate, and not he alone, had determined the course of events.

Since we know that Raskolnikov not only willed, but, in a sense, long planned the murder, we sense the narrator's irony at the expense of even the more mature Raskolnikov. Raskolnikov's preoccupation with the morality of crime and the psychology of the criminal extends many months before the action proper begins. In Part One, Chapter Six, he recalls overhearing, six weeks earlier, a conversation between a student and an officer about the morality of murdering the old pawnbroker; he also recalls being superstitiously struck by the fact that he had just returned from her and had left with the very same idea. Though it seems that Raskolnikov had chosen his victim only a month and a half before the start of the novel, we know that the moral justification for the con-templated crime was laid out in an article that he finished before he left the university — half a year before the actual murder. But even more astonishing is Raskolnikov's confession to Dunya that he had explained all his ideas to his former fiancée, who died over a year before the events of the novel.

Yet, even if the events surrounding the murder were coincidental, the murder itself was inevitable. If it had not been Alyona Ivanovna, it would have been someone else. Another month or so locked up in his close garret, hungry, depressed, and feverish, Raskolnikov would have honed his casuistry so sharp as to rationalize the murder of one far less physically and morally repulsive than the old pawnbroker. No wonder a note of irony exists in the narrator's statement that Raskolnikov believed that one incident, though really not very unusual, determined his fate.

The narrator alludes to the reminiscences of other characters too. Though these reminiscences are not treated with the same irony as Raskol-nikov's, they seem to cover the same time period. For example, Razu-mikhin remembers for his whole life the minute in the corridor when Raskolnikov charges him with the care of his sister and mother. Zametov recalls the strangeness of his meeting with Raskolnikov in the Crystal Palace, and Sonya remembers the moment when Raskolnikov first confesses to her that he murdered Lizaveta: "Later on, long afterwards, when she recalled that minute it seemed strange to her and she even wondered why she had actually seen at once that there could be no doubt about it." (318) Phrased almost exactly like Raskolnikov's, Sonya's recollection projects her life as far into the future as his. What is more, the very applicability of the same temporal system to Sonya and other characters guarantees its objective reality for the novel as a whole. It is not merely a device to emphasize the confusion of the experiencing Raskolnikov; it is an integral part of the novel's rhetorical structure.

These reminiscence passages may in fact even indicate that the whole novel is a confession as related to a third party. Take, for example, the brief reminiscence passage that introduces the scene in which the peasant Nikolay bursts in on Porfiry Petrovich and Raskolnikov and confesses to the murder: "Later on when he [Raskolnikov] recalled this minute, this is how he saw everything." (272) Can we conclude from this statement that the narrator perhaps is a writer to whom a reformed Raskolnikov has recounted all his experiences and to whom he has given permission to write his biography as a lesson to others? Can *Crime and Punishment* be Dostoevsky's initial attempt at writing the first part of that project so dear to his heart, *The Life of a Great Sinner*? The rather far-reaching implications of such a view are indeed intriguing; certainly it is an area which demands further study.

In addition to projecting the events well past the frame of the novel proper, the reminiscence passages foreshadow the epilogue, which in its turn makes explicit the implications of Raskolnikov's recollections. Thus together with the epilogue, they form a coherent temporal and ironic system that runs through the entire novel and answers questions only implied in the novel proper: What is Raskolnikov's fate? Is there any hope for those who have been corrupted by pride and the rationalistic heresies of the West? Raskolnikov, after all, is more than an isolated murderer or even a social type; he is a symbol of one stage in the spiritual and intellectual development of man. He is Dostoevsky's most successful attempt at creating not a superman but an everyman.

The relation between the epilogue and the reminiscence passages is complex. Although we are told from the very beginning that the hero is recalling events long after they have occurred, only gradually do we realize that the reminiscence passages take us far beyond the time of the epilogue into the nebulous temporal realm which the narrator says belongs to a different story. Therefore, they presuppose not only Raskolnikov's imprisonment, but the long process of his regeneration as well.

Yet the process is far from complete. The reminiscent Raskolnikov still does not possess the narrator's insight into the crime and its causes; for this knowledge can come only after the many years of suffering that the narrator prophesies for him on the last page of the epilogue.

Raskolnikov's regeneration, of course, is not made explicit in the reminiscence statements; it is implied and then only when seen in conjunction with other scenes and statements in the novel proper. And this could hardly be otherwise. To insist on Raskolnikov's resurrection in the reminiscence passages would reduce the psychological suspense in the novel proper and destroy the effect of Raskolnikov's miraculous, if not unexpected, conversion in the epilogue. When taken together with certain events and scenes, however, the reminiscence passages form a more than suggestive outline of Raskolnikov's fate, in fact, an obvious enough one to make the epilogue a summary — what it probably was intended to be — and not a shock. We know of Raskolnikov's latent religious traits: his prayers as a little boy; his inexplicable feeling for St. Isaac's Cathedral; his literal belief in the New Jerusalem; and his desire to hear of the raising of Lazarus from the dead. We also witness his compulsive need to confess, if not expiate, his crime: his fainting at the police station; his challenge to the peasants at Alyona Ivanovna's; his disclosures to Sonya; and finally his confession to Ilya Petrovich. We are also aware at all times of the almost allegorical role of Raskolnikov's saving grace, Sonya Marmeladov; and we sense that her efforts will not be in vain. These scenes add flesh to the vague intimations of the reminiscence statements about Raskolnikov's future. But the effect is reciprocal. When viewed in terms of the double time-perspective created by the reminiscence passages, all the symbolism, events, and episodes pointing to Raskolnikov's transformation in the epilogue achieve greater artistic credibility. The very fact that we know the remembering Raskolnikov is significantly different from the experiencing one makes the hope that Sonya holds out to him a possibility that the reader must seriously entertain. Our sensibilities are prepared — if ever so slightly — for Raskolnikov's rebirth in the epilogue.

If the main function of the reminiscence passages is to foreshadow the epilogue, what then is the function of the epilogue itself? Is it there merely to confirm our intuitions, or does it add to our understanding of Raskolnikov's personality and the implications of his fate? And how important a role does the narrator play in the epilogue? What, for example, does he do in the epilogue that he does not do in the novel proper? Most critics have understandably shown little concern for the narrator in the epilogue; they have in general been dissatisfied with the events themselves, and consequently have seen little need to examine how they are presented.[5] Ernest J. Simmons, who holds that Raskolnikov's conversion is insufficiently motivated, even speculates that the epilogue may be little more than Dostoevsky's attempt to satisfy his audience's need for a moralistic ending.[6] Most critics are obviously objecting to Dostoevsky's "failure" to present Raskolnikov's conversion in as detailed and psychological a manner as his plan for the murder, his execution of it, and his ordeal after it. But since a miraculous conversion can hardly be so presented, what the critics of the epilogue are in effect saying is that the conversion itself lacks verisimilitude: it is unbelievable that the proud and defiant Raskolnikov of the novel proper could experience such a turnabout — Sonya Marmeladov notwithstanding.

In answer to this criticism, I have noted in this and previous chapters some of the structural, if not psychological, devices that Dostoevsky uses to motivate the epilogue. Scenes, facts, and statements from the very beginning foreshadow the events to come. In this section, I shall confine my discussion to differences in the narrative structure of the epilogue and

---

[5] I know of no Soviet critic who has thought the epilogue artistically satisfying. But Western critics have not been especially pleased with the epilogue either. See, for example, John Middleton Murry, *Fyodor Dostoevsky: A Critical Study* (London: Martin Secker, 1923), pp. 122–3; Julius Meier-Graefe, *Dostoevsky: The Man and His Work*, trans. by Herbert H. Marks (New York: Harcourt, 1928), pp. 134–8, 140; Ernest J. Simmons, *Dostoevsky: The Making of a Novelist* (1940; rpt. London: John Lehmann, 1950), pp. 152–5. Konstantin Mochulsky, *Dostoevsky: His Life and Work*, trans. by Michael A. Minihan (Princeton: Princeton Univ. Press, 1967), p. 312, on the whole an adherent of Dostoevsky's Christian anthropology, calls the epilogue "a pious lie". There are also those who believe all epilogues are artistically inadequate. V. B. Šklovskij, *Povesti o proze: Razmyšlenija i razbory* (M.: GIXL, 1966), II, 220–1, maintains novelists use epilogues because they are unable to complete their stories adequately. Joseph Warren Beach, *The Twentieth Century Novel: Studies in Technique* (New York: Appleton, 1932), p. 249, says that "the twentieth century reader does not relish this [the epilogue's] sketchy messing about with future events; he does not care to be told how each character received the due reward of his virtuous life. He likes his curtain neat and definitive." The narrator's remarks in *A Friend of the Family* on the epilogue of that work indicate that Dostoevsky must have been well aware of the pitfalls of epilogues, and thus we may assume that he had a good reason for including them in his two greatest works, *Crime and Punishment* and *The Brothers Karamazov.* "My story is ended. The lovers were united and the spirit of goodness, as it were, reigned supreme in the house in the person of Foma Fomich. Here one could make many fitting observations; but, in essence, all such observations are now completely superfluous. That, at least, is my opinion. In lieu of any such observations, I shall say only a few words about the subsequent fate of all the heroes of my story: without this, as is well known no novel can end, and this is even prescribed by the rules." F. M. Dostoevskij, *Sobranie sočinenij* (M.: GIXL, 1956–8), II, 631.

[6] Simmons, p. 152.

the novel proper, in order to clarify the organic ties between the two, in particular the nature of Raskolnikov's transition from the old life to the new.

The narrational commentary of the first one-and-a-half chapters of the epilogue differs little from that of the novel proper. In the first chapter, the narrator describes Raskolnikov's trial and recounts in chronological order: Sonya's following him to Siberia, Dunya and Razumikhin's marriage, and Pulkheria Alexandrovna's derangement and death. Just as in the novel proper, the narrator from time to time treats his material with varying degrees of irony. Raskolnikov's trial is a good example. Although he loved to attend trials, especially those involving murder, Dostoevsky remained a lifelong skeptic of the Western-type jury system, which was established in Russia as a consequence of the great reforms of 1864. This skepticism was, of course, to receive the full brunt of Dostoevsky's satiric genius in the last part of *The Brothers Karamazov*; but it is also present in his treatment of the lawyers' and judges' attempts to understand Raskolnikov's crime.

In the end, several (especially the psychologists) even admitted the possibility that he really didn't look into the purse, and therefore didn't even know what was in it; and not knowing its contents, simply hid it under a stone. But it was from this fact that they concluded that the crime itself could not have occurred other than in a condition of temporary insanity, that is to say, under the influence of a maniacal compulsion to kill and steal, without any goal or calculation for gain. Here by the way, the latest fashionable theory of temporary insanity, which is used so often in our day with regard to certain criminals, worked in Raskolnikov's favor. (411–12)

The narrator's irony is obvious. Temporary insanity, at least from a psychological point of view, seems a shallow explanation for the complex mental attitudes that led to the crime — it is a fashionable theory, an abstraction, and by its very nature, incapable of accurately describing a living process. Moreover, Raskolnikov was not temporarily insane, unless one argues that all men who commit murder are insane at the moment of the crime. If, on the other hand, insanity is taken to mean a distorted view of reality, then Raskolnikov must be considered insane not temporarily, but throughout most of the novel. The psychologists are able to pigeon-hole Raskolnikov's case on the least substantial of evidence, whereas the novelist, even with direct access to the consciousness of his hero, has left the motivation — at least the purely psychological aspect of it — basically unresolved. The narrator also undercuts the way the psychologists have arrived at their theory: they have interpreted Raskolnikov's failure to look inside the purse as evidence that he was not in full possession of his faculties, as if the murder alone did not furnish sufficient reason. And yet it is perhaps understandable why they come to such superficial conclusions; they, after all, have no real knowledge of Raskolnikov's motivation: Raskolnikov has not killed to rob; he has robbed to kill.

Although the narrator's commentary is present throughout the description of the trial, it is relatively inconspicuous. It does not differ significantly from the subtler forms of irony in the novel proper. What is more, there is very little commentary in the rest of the chapter. Most of what the narrator reports about Razumikhin, Dunya, Pulkheria Alexandrovna, Sonya, and Raskolnikov is factual. He shows some compassion for the deranged Pulkheria Alexandrovna and presents the actions of Dunya, Razumikhin, and Sonya in a positive light; but no more so than in previous chapters. In fact, the summaries here are some of the most non-evaluative in the novel.

The first half of Chapter Two is also like the novel proper with regard to commentary. The narrator speaks to us at length about Raskolnikov, but he generally refrains from openly censuring him. We are told that he initially fails to fit in with life in the penal colony, but this is a fact that anyone at the prison could confirm. Yet the narrator's frequent criticism can be sensed. While ostensibly transcribing only consciousness, he constantly chips away at his hero's inflated picture of his self-inflicted suffering.

> He had been ill for a long time; but it was neither the life of a convict, the food, his shaven head, nor his ragged clothing that crushed him. O! What did he care about all that suffering and torment! On the contrary, he was even glad about the work: physical exhaustion at least gave him a few hours of peaceful sleep. And what was food to him — this thin cabbage soup with its cockroaches? During his former life as a student he often didn't have even that. His clothing was warm and adapted to his way of life. As for the fetters, he hardly even felt them. Should he be ashamed of his shaven head and parti-colored jacket? Before whom? Sonya? Sonya was afraid of him; could he possibly be ashamed before her?
>
> And yet, he was ashamed even before Sonya, whom he tortured for this by treating her roughly and contemptuously. (417)

The elements of oral speech — the bragging, exclamations, and rhetorical questions — all indicate that this is narrated consciousness. Despite the humiliations and hardships of prison life, Raskolnikov is still the same man. The fetters, after all, cannot crush his spirit, nor can they dent his exalted self-image; for did he not tell Porfiry Petrovich that "those of great heart and intelligence are always bound to endure pain and suffering"; that "the truly great men ... must experience great sadness on earth." (206)

Yet, though the passage is told from Raskolnikov's point of view, the narrator is discernible, mimicking Raskolnikov for ironic effect. Raskolnikov's dismissal of the hardships and degradations of prison life is prideful boasting. He pretends to be unashamed of his shaven head and parti-colored jacket; but as the narrator is quick to point out — in a remark that puts all that precedes in an ironic light — Raskolnikov was ashamed even before Sonya, and tortured her because he was conscious of it. The use of this technique in the epilogue indicates that even at this point the hero has undergone no significant change. Subtle, biting irony remains the mode most appropriate for the still unrepentant and boundlessly proud Raskolnikov.

In some of the passages that follow, the narrator increases his distance from the hero, presenting Raskolnikov's thoughts in interior monologue. Raskolnikov is still unrepentant and convinced as firmly as ever that he is perishing senselessly; that what he has done is a crime only from a legal point of view, and then only because his deed was not crowned with success. He still believes as before that might makes right: "But those men were successful, and so *they were right*, and I was a failure, and thus I didn't have the right to permit myself such a step." (418) Just as in the previous passage, the narrator immediately undercuts his hero's position after transcribing his thoughts: "And only in this respect did he acknowledge his crime, that he had failed and confessed." (418) Once again, the narrator censures Raskolnikov's perverted scale of values. To further emphasize the narrator's criticism, Dostoevsky sets off the brief comment by making it into an independent paragraph. This is undeniably strong commentary, but it is far from unique. The narrator treats Raskolnikov in much the same way in the novel proper.

Yet on the second page of this last chapter in the novel (in fact, immediately after the narrator's remark discussed above) there is a passage of an entirely different order.

He was also tormented by another question: why had he not killed himself? Why, when he was standing above the river had he chosen to confess? Could the will to live be so strong and so difficult to over-come? Svidrigaylov, who feared death, had overcome it.

He asked himself this tormenting question and was incapable of realizing that even then, when he was standing looking over the river he had perhaps pre-sensed a profound falsity in himself and in his convictions. He didn't realize that this presentiment could be the harbinger of a change in his life, of his resurrection, of a new view on life. (419)

First the narrator tells us that the beginnings of Raskolnikov's rebirth and his new view on life were already present long before he confessed the crime to the police. But even here he is not perfectly explicit; he does not say that Raskolnikov "pre-sensed" the falsity in himself, but "per-haps pre-sensed" it. This reservation, however, is somewhat neutralized by the next statement, in which he speaks explicitly about resurrection and the new life — the dominant motif of the last few pages of the epilogue. Not only the content, but the tone is entirely different from what we have seen before. We immediately sense that Raskolnikov's resurrection and his new view on life represent a dramatic change for the better. One could argue that the narrator's references to Raskolnikov's rebirth are but facts and not explicit commentary, but few can fail to note the approval in the narrator's tone and the criticism that the word *lož'* — which in Russian combines the meaning of "falsehood" and the force of "lie" — stamps on Raskolnikov's former convictions.

In the last two pages of the novel, however, the commentary becomes perfectly explicit. It seems as if the narrator no longer feels the need to conceal, even partially, his feeling about Raskolnikov's changed outlook. Again the theme of resurrection is sounded: "They wanted to speak, but could not. Tears stood in their eyes. They were both pale and thin, but in these sick pale faces already shone the dawn of a new future of a full resurrection into a new life. Love had resurrected them, the heart of one contained infinite sources of life for the heart of the other." (422) What is surprising here is not what is said, but who is saying it. The narrator has not shown his sympathy for these ideas in such an explicit form since Sonya's reading of Lazarus. But this passage is much more than an echo; it provides the Lazarus scene with a sense of completion; of fulfilled prophecy. Sonya's most cherished hopes have been realized; and what is more, Raskolnikov's arguments against her faith in God have been crushed when he attempts to consider her point of view. The raising of Lazarus has become a vital reality for nineteenth-century Petersburg, and thus for all time.

The narrator seems to exult in Raskolnikov's resurrection just as he had shown sympathy in the Lazarus scene for Sonya's faith; and, as in the Lazarus scene, the tone is perfectly harmonized with the message: it is completely devoid of that irony with which Raskolnikov is treated throughout the novel. If the Lazarus passage foreshadows these explicit statements in the epilogue, then they in turn give the earlier prophecies greater artistic credibility.

The narrator's most outspoken commentary on Raskolnikov occurs on the last page of the epilogue. Here he sides with feeling and emotion over sterile logic: open approval of the new Raskolnikov is evident in every word.

> But on that evening he was unable to reflect or concentrate on anything for any length of time: he could not in fact analyze anything consciously, he only felt. Life had taken the place of dialectics. And something entirely different had to work itself out in his consciousness. ... He didn't even know that the new life would not be given to him for nothing, that it would have to be bought dearly, and paid for by a great sacrifice in the future. (423)

This type of commentary on Raskolnikov naturally raises questions about Dostoevsky's artistic judgment. Did he fail to sense the inappropriateness of such praise; or is it a device with a function no less important than the subtle and for the most part implicit commentary in the novel proper. A close examination of the text shows that the change in the narrator's treatment of Raskolnikov perfectly fits the function of the epilogue.

Although there has been very little theoretical work done on the epilogue as a narrative device, it is generally assumed that it should not be structurally necessary to the story proper. In practice, the function of most epilogues is to make explicit what in the novel proper may have been only implied. But an epilogue is not only an explanatory conclusion, it is a conclusion that differs from the novel both tonally and structurally; for everything in it is designed to give a note of finality and a sense of resolution to that which has preceded. It also acts as a safeguard ensuring that what was implied in the novel proper is not misunderstood — some might even say, and it has been said about *Crime and Punishment*, that it is a concession to less perceptive readers.[7] In any event, it is the part where all things are made plain — and, in this regard, the epilogue of *Crime and Punishment* is no exception.

Perhaps the most striking stylistic characteristic of the epilogue setting

---

[7] Simmons, p. 152; Mochulsky, p. 312.

it off from the novel proper is its preponderance of summary. Whereas most of the scenes in the novel proper are dramatically conceived, the epilogue is in large part devoted to recounting what happens after Raskolnikov gives himself up to the police. Although it contains a considerable amount of narrated speech, and even a passage of interior monologue, it includes only three lines of dialogue, which perhaps explains why readers have felt the epilogue to differ so radically from everything that precedes it. The heavy use of summary in the epilogue is deliberate: it is the only way the narrator can concisely bring the histories of his major characters up to date, especially those whose fate is important to the thematic structure of the novel. Here again the epilogue holds no surprises, but rather makes explicit what was implied in the novel proper: Sonya follows Raskolnikov to Siberia and becomes instrumental in his resurrection; Dunya and Razumikhin get married; and Pulkheria Alexandrovna dies from grief over her son.

The temporal structure of the epilogue is also affected by the summary technique. Whereas the first six parts of the novel take only twelve days, the epilogue (barely one twenty-fifth of the novel in length) takes over nine months — long enough evidently for Raskolnikov to be reborn. The pace of the epilogue is leisurely; the events are not cramped as they so often are in the novel proper. There are also long periods about which we are told nothing. Whereas in the novel proper Dostoevsky is constantly reminding us of the exact time and place of events, in the epilogue we are introduced to a special temporal realm more conducive to the eternal verities of the Bible than to the existential realities of slum life of nineteenth-century Petersburg: "Freedom was there, there other people lived, so utterly unlike those on this side of the river that it seems as though with them time had stood still, and the age of Abraham and his flocks was still present." (422)

The presentation of Raskolnikov's psychology in the epilogue also contrasts sharply with that of the novel proper. The first chapter hardly treats of his psychology at all. Much of it concerns Razumikhin, Dunya, and Pulkheria Alexandrovna, and the parts that deal with Raskolnikov touch only his outward behavior. The narrator's description of the trial for example focuses on the judicial process and not on the psychology of the accused; and our knowledge of Raskolnikov's first days in prison is restricted to Sonya's letters, which, as the narrator says, "were full of the most prosaic actuality, the simplest and clearest description of every circumstance of Raskolnikov's life as a convict. ... There were only facts, his own words, that is, and detailed reports of his health. ..." (416)

The concluding chapter, with the exception of the first few pages, treats of Raskolnikov's psychology in only the most general terms, contrasting sharply with the novel proper, in which the hero's every act and thought is subjected to detailed interior analysis. In this last chapter the narrator summarizes Raskolnikov's observations on prison life and the behavior of his fellow inmates, but tells us little about his inner experiences.

The conclusion contains a dream that also differs significantly from the ones within the novel. First of all, it is not an experiential dream at all — in fact, Raskolnikov is not even a participant.[8] Whereas his other dreams are so vivid and subtly integrated into the novel that the reader often feels that he is experiencing not a dream but reality, the dream of the epilogue is a remembered one. Moreover, it is not a single dream at all, but a composite of an unspecified number of dreams presumably with nearly identical content. Like much of the material in the epilogue, it is a summary; but it is a summary of a very special kind; for it represents the narrator's most explicit statement on the causes of Raskolnikov's illness and crime. Raskolnikov has fallen victim to rationalism, an infectious disease, which eventually results in the death of all but a few pure souls whose fate it is to found a new race of men. Thus, the dream reveals the underlying ideology of *Crime and Punishment*, and as such fulfils the epilogue's prime function: to spell out the implications of the novel proper.

The remainder of the chapter relates Raskolnikov's feelings of hope renewed — a psychological state that, of course, comes about only in the epilogue.

> And what were all, *all* those torments of the past! Everything, even his crime, even his sentence and exile seemed to him now in the first rush of emotion something external and strange, something which hadn't even happened to him. ... Life had taken the place of dialectics. ... But that is the beginning of a new story, of the gradual renewal of a man, of his gradual rebirth, his gradual transition from one world into another, his acquaintance with a new hitherto absolutely undreamed-of reality. This could constitute the theme of a new story — but our present one has come to an end. (423)

This, admittedly, is no longer the psychology of the old unrepentant

---

[8] For a discussion of the differences between Raskolnikov's dream in the epilogue and his four dreams in the novel proper, see J. Thomas Shaw, "Raskol'nikov's Dreams," *Slavic and East European Journal*, 17 (1973), 139–44.

Raskolnikov; nor is his psychology presented in the same way. The narrator says that Raskolnikov is a new man, and says it with obvious approval. The change in technique corresponds to the change in Raskolnikov himself. But the change is not as abrupt, improbable, or poorly motivated, even from a psychological point of view, as critics have made it out to be. The criticism that Raskolnikov's religious side is not enough developed in the novel proper fails to take into consideration that Raskolnikov's religious traits must be latent. If they were not, he would never have entered upon so destructive a path in the first place.

That these traits are latent does not mean, however, that they are not forcefully implied and in some cases dramatically presented. Scenes like Raskolnikov's dream of childhood, his desire to hear of the raising of Lazarus, and his literal belief in the New Jerusalem all establish this other side of his personality; and they would be meaningless if they did not do so.

The detractors of the epilogue have further failed to realize that Raskolnikov's miraculous conversion must be understood in both metaphysical and practical terms.[9] Raskolnikov is not transformed in the epilogue into a saint. At most, the direction of his life has been changed. From a metaphysical point of view, this is indeed a miracle and enough justification to call Raskolnikov a new man; but practically speaking, he is far from complete recovery, which, as the narrator explicitly states, is in the distant future and will be paid for dearly. Raskolnikov's feeling of new life most clearly manifests itself in his appreciation of Sonya, who has patiently seen him through many crises, without unduly pressing him with religion. But it is inaccurate to call his rebirth in the epilogue a religious conversion; for he does not exchange his former atheistic views for Sonya's Orthodoxy, but begins to live emotionally rather than analytically. "Couldn't her beliefs possibly be mine now? Her feelings and her aspirations, at least ...?" (423) The phrase "at least" indicates that Raskolnikov dismisses the possibility of immediately accepting Sonya's religious views. He asks instead whether he can share her feelings — especially her great love and devotion; and her aspirations — her hope for their future happiness. Whether Raskolnikov can ever accept Sonya's beliefs is a question that the narrator has relegated to another time and place — and to another story. Raskolnikov is symbolically reformed in the epilogue; but in terms of the world, as the narrator states, his renewal

---

[9] For an interesting discussion of the nature of Raskolnikov's conversion in the epilogue, see A. Boyce Gibson, *The Religion of Dostoevsky* (London: SCM Press Limited, 1973), pp. 88–103.

will be a slow and gradual one, one which could only constitute a new tale, and one which would require the detailed presentation of Raskolnikov's psychology, so characteristic of the novel proper.

We could, of course, accept the events of the epilogue and still have reservations about the way they are presented. The narrator's almost ecstatic approval of the new path Raskolnikov is embarking upon may constitute for some readers a shock greater than Raskolnikov's renewal itself. But if the epilogue is designed to clarify what in the novel proper is chiefly implicit, then the narrator's explicit and strongly worded commentary in it becomes not only appropriate, but essential.

CHAPTER 10

THE HIGHER POINT OF VIEW

The last few chapters, in which I have focused on the various methods used by the narrator to influence the reader's judgment of the characters and events, are not to be construed as an argument that *Crime and Punishment* is more subjectively told than most other novels written during the same period. Even if objectivity is defined as the absence from the novel of a narrator who generalizes about life and who comments in his own person on the merits and foibles of his characters, *Crime and Punishment* must still be considered one of the most objective novels of the second half of the nineteenth century.

Though Dostoevsky neither depersonalizes his narrator nor reduces his function to the transcription of consciousness, he generally lets the story tell itself. Third-person narration significantly speeds up the flow of events while the extensive use of narrated consciousness and interior monologue lend an objective aura to the narrator's presentation of Raskolnikov's psychology. Furthermore, the great amount of dialogue in the novel gives it to some extent the appearance and feel of a real play.[1] As Percy Lubbock might say, by successfully making us suspend our disbelief, Dostoevsky compels us to take his story as something shown, not told.

Indeed, one has only to compare *Crime and Punishment* with the most prominent novels written at the same time to see how objective it is for its age. It is certainly more objective than the novels of Dickens, Balzac, and George Eliot. Tolstoy and Turgenev, Dostoevsky's major rivals in his own country, wrote no novels so "impersonal" as *Crime and Punishment*. Even Flaubert's *Madame Bovary*, still much praised for its

---

[1] This is one of the central theses of Vyacheslav Ivanov's pre-revolutionary *Freedom and the Tragic Life: A Study in Dostoevsky*, trans. by Norman Cameron (New York: Noonday, 1957). In the last twelve years it has become widely accepted in the Soviet Union, influenced, no doubt, by M. M. Bakhtin's *Problemy poètiki Dostoevskogo*, 2nd ed. (M.: Sov. pisatel', 1963), though Bakhtin's thesis was presented in virtually the same form in the first (1929) edition of the book.

objectivity, employs a more subjective and personal narrator. Though the narrator in *Crime and Punishment* from time to time indulges in philosophical generalizations, he does so far less than his counterpart in *Madame Bovary*. The two novels also differ in their treatment of the characters' inner lives, especially in the transcription of consciousness. In *Crime and Punishment*, the feelings and thoughts of the characters are, on the whole, recorded in their own language. In *Madame Bovary*, however, the polished style of the narrator's prose shows through whenever he must transcribe the vulgar minds of Charles and Emma.

It can be argued that the transcription of consciousness appears more objective in *Crime and Punishment* because the characters are articulate and rather close to the narrator's intellectual level. The objectivity of some of Henry James's novels, for example, may have more to do with the narrator's and characters' similar sensibilities than with James's declared intention of filtering all the events through the consciousness of a central intelligence. But the narrator's language in *Madame Bovary* goes far beyond a neutral rendering of the characters' psyches; in fact, in places it becomes involved in elaborate metaphors strangely incommensurate with the sensations and thoughts that they are meant to convey. The metaphoric method of transcribing consciousness, we have seen, is also present in *Crime and Punishment*; but it is used only sparingly. The following passage, which brings out Emma's growing disillusionment with Charles, is typical of Flaubert's method of presenting Emma's thoughts.

> Yet if Charles had wished it, if he had guessed, if his look had but once met her thought, it seemed to her that a sudden abundance would have broken loose from her heart, as the fruit falls from a tree when shaken by a hand. But as the intimacy of their life increased, a profound indifference sundered her from him.
>
> Charles's conversation was flat as a street pavement, and every one's ideas marched down it in their everyday garb, without exciting emotion, laughter, or thought. He had never had the curiosity, he said, while he lived at Rouen, to go to the theater to see the actors from Paris. He could neither swim, nor fence, nor shoot, and one day he could not explain some term of horsemanship to her that she had come across in a novel.[2]

---

[2] The translations from *Madame Bovary* are those of Paul de Man in *Madame Bovary* (New York: Norton, 1965), p. 29, revised as appropriate on the basis of the French text in *Oeuvres complètes de Gustave Flaubert*, I (Paris: Club de l'Honnête Homme, 1971), pp. 83–4. Further references in the text are first to page numbers in the Norton edition, then to page numbers in the French edition.

Emma feels betrayed: she had thought that in marriage at last she would realize her most cherished dreams. But Charles is no Prince Charming. To Emma's dismay, he does not wear a black velvet coat with long tails, nor does he own a Swiss chalet with a balcony. To show that Emma believes she is not at fault for her growing dissatisfaction with Charles, Flaubert employs several elegant comparisons. He likens what Emma's warm and full response would have been — had Charles made the proper gesture — to the fruit falling from a tree when shaken by a hand. Certainly, it is not Emma who makes this comparison; at least it strikes us as being quite different from the thousands of clichés that she has imbibed in her reading of romantic and sentimental fiction. But one can never be sure. However, the last sentence of the paragraph speaking of Emma's growing indifference to Charles clearly represents the point of view of the evaluating narrator.

The second paragraph contains two contrasting methods of transcription. The last two sentences, for example, represent rather accurately what Emma is thinking; it is conceivable that she might even use the very same words: "He had never had the curiosity ... while he lived in Rouen, to go to the theater to see the actors from Paris." In the first sentence, however, the narrator's description of Charles's conversation can hardly be ascribed to Emma. Both the structure of the sentence and the content of the comparison are beyond her. For, at this point in the novel, the pavement symbolizes to Emma, not the crassness of the city, but its cultural refinements. Later she will even take pride in walking down the streets of Rouen on her lover's arm — it is only towards the end of the novel that she realizes that the city is no more a solution to her problems than is Charles. Stylistically the comparison also points to the narrator's presence. Flaubert realizes the metaphor by having everybody's ideas march down the flat pavement of Charles's conversation. And the three carefully placed nouns at the end of the sentence bring the thought to a close with a finely tuned cadence.

Often Flaubert makes no attempt to conceal the personality of the narrator in the description of Emma's consciousness: "As for the memory of Rodolphe she stored it at the very bottom of her heart, and it remained there more solemn and still than a pharaoh's mummy in a vault. A vapor escaped from this great embalmed love, that, penetrating through everything, perfumed with tenderness the immaculate atmosphere in which she longed to live." (155; 239) This may be parody, but one suspects that it reflects the narrator's romanticism more than Emma's sentimentality. Although passages like these do not occur on every page in *Madame*

Bovary, there are enough of them to make the novel less objectively told than *Crime and Punishment*.

If we consider *Madame Bovary* as our test for objectivity, then *Crime and Punishment* is indeed objective. In fact, it is hard to conceive of a more objectively told novel, given the period when it was written; for most nineteenth-century novels contain, as part of their basic structure, a significantly personalized, if not dramatized, narrator. The astonishing fact about the narrator in *Crime and Punishment* is that Dostoevsky so deftly wove him into the novel that he is sometimes overlooked altogether. Only a certain amount of critical probing reveals that he indeed carries out all the traditional functions of the omniscient author.

The narrator of *Crime and Punishment* does not merely comment on the action and characters; he provides the novel with a unity of vision often lacking in works done in a more consciously objective and impersonal style. Symbolism, plot, and characterization are not the only fictional elements that give a novel unity and make it throb with life. Perhaps just as vital is that accent in the novelist's voice, that dramatic presence, that both E. M. Forster[3] and Wolfgang Kayser[4] have argued is so important.

Scholars and critics of *Crime and Punishment* have repeatedly praised the novel for its remarkable unity, a unity which is all the more striking when compared with Dostoevsky's other major works.[5] Most commentators have argued that this unity results from the author's almost exclusive concentration on the hero. Mochulsky, perhaps the most articulate proponent of this position, sees Raskolnikov as the dynamic center from which all other elements of plot, theme, and characterization receive their definition.[6] Though this interpretation of the novel's unity is

---

[3] *Aspects of the Novel* (New York: Harcourt, 1927), pp. 125–6.

[4] *Entstehung und Krise des modernen Romans*, 2nd ed. (Stuttgart: J. B. Metzlersche Verlagsbuchhandlung, 1955), p. 34: "Ein für den Roman wesentliches Formprinzip. . .ist der Erzähler, vielleicht das wesentlichste."

[5] See Joseph Warren Beach, *The Twentieth Century Novel: Studies in Technique* (New York: Appleton, 1932), pp. 157, 161; G. I. Čulkov, *Kak rabotal Dostoevskij* (M.: Sov. pisatel', 1939), pp. 141–2; Konstantin Mochulsky, *Dostoevsky: His Life and Work*, trans. by Michael A. Minihan (Princeton: Princeton Univ. Press, 1967), pp. 298–300; V. B. Šklovskij, *Za i protiv: Zametki o Dostoevskom* (M.: Sov. pisatel', 1957), pp. 173–4; L. P. Grossman, "Dostoevskij — xudožnik," in *Tvorčestvo F. M. Dostoevskogo*, ed. by N. L. Stepanov (M.: AN SSSR, 1959), p. 392; F. I. Evnin, "Roman 'Prestuplenie i nakazanie,'" in *Tvorčestvo F. M. Dostoevskogo*, pp. 165–6; M. M. Baxtin, pp. 20–31; V. I. Ètov, "Priemy psixologičeskogo analiza v romane 'Prestuplenie i nakazanie,'" *Vestnik Moskovskogo universiteta*, Serija 10, Filologija, No. 3 (1967), p. 3.

[6] Mochulsky, p. 298.

rather obvious, it does not in any way lessen its validity: *Crime and Punishment* was conceived as the story of one man and one fate, and critical opinion has accepted this view.

For some scholars this has been too easy an answer. L. P. Grossman, for example, has shown that although *Crime and Punishment* leaves us with the impression of a marvelously unified whole, it is actually an amalgam of heterogeneous material. Aspects of the psychological sketch, the murder mystery, and the Gothic novel combine freely in it with confessions, Biblical passages, letters, and philosophical debates. How could Dostoevsky, he asks, so effortlessly and successfully combine the most disparate and seemingly incompatible elements of both fictional and nonfictional narrative? The answer, he contends, is to be found in plot, not characterization. Dostoevsky creates artistic unity by subjecting the heterogeneous material of his story to the dynamism of his plot. In this way, he is able to construct a novel of great metaphysical significance around the sensational intrigues of the *roman feuilleton*. To Grossman, the breath-taking speed of events does not permit the reader to focus on the individual building blocks of structure. It is almost as if the plot is a crucible in which the elements fuse, losing their original form and function.[7] Indeed, anyone who has been caught up in the plot of *Crime and Punishment* can easily appreciate Grossman's original hypothesis. Though it is difficult to demonstrate, it is an interesting and much-needed complement to Mochulsky's perhaps too one-sided interpretation.

The boldest approach to *Crime and Punishment*, however, is taken by Bakhtin, who sees its unity not in the traditional forms of plot and characterization, but in its polyphonic point of view. As I outlined earlier, Bakhtin holds that in all of Dostoevsky's novels after *Notes from the Underground*, each character represents an equally valid view of the world, which is in no way subordinated to that of the narrator or author. The unity of *Crime and Punishment* is thus a parodoxical unity of diversity, even discord, the unity of a never-ending dialectic of world views, each groping towards its own understanding of reality. It thus is a dynamic unity, for it is a process, not an idea.[8]

Bakhtin's critics, however, have argued convincingly that the voices in Dostoevsky's novels are by no means of equal validity or independence.[9]

---

[7] L. P. Grossman, *Poètika Dostoevskogo* (M.: Gos. akad. xud. nauk, 1925), pp. 74–80; and "Dostoevskij — xudožnik," pp. 371–85.

[8] Baxtin, pp. 20–1.

[9] See A. V. Lunačarskij, "O 'mnogogolosnosti' Dostoevskogo," in *F. M. Dostoevskij v russkoj kritike: Sbornik statej*, ed. by A. A. Belkin (M.: GIXL, 1956),

Symbolism, plot, and characterization in *Crime and Punishment*, as in most of his novels, are all subordinated to a carefully worked out higher frame of reference. Nevertheless, Bakhtin's theories at least force us to come to grips with the role of the narrator as a unifying element in the novel. For neither Grossman's theory of plot nor Mochulsky's theory of character fully explains the novel's unity — especially in light of the epilogue.

In direct contrast to Bakhtin's thesis, it has been the object of this study to demonstrate to what extent the points of view of the characters in *Crime and Punishment* are subordinated to the higher point of view of the narrator. The underlying evaluative structure of *Crime and Punishment* is, to be sure, found in the symbolism and other devices of characterization and plot that may be ascribed to the implied author. But Dostoevsky makes use of the personalized narrator time and again to convey these norms to the reader. Precisely because he does not recede into the background, he can serve as a sort of central intelligence subordinating all the points of view to his own. Ultimately it is to this personalized higher point of view that *Crime and Punishment* owes its remarkable unity.

This unity is greatly enhanced by the narrator's ability to use the epilogue as a means not only of making explicit what was implied in the novel proper, but of synthesizing the heterogeneous material of the story. For it is only in the epilogue that the underlying vision alluded to by various means throughout the novel is finally made explicit, and it is only in the epilogue that the past, present, and future are shown to be a carefully laid-out pattern of a higher point of view. The epilogue concludes the narrator's morality play; it is time for him to reveal the full extent of his knowledge. And that includes knowledge of all that has taken place and all that is to come.

The higher point of view of *Crime and Punishment* comprises not only a system of values by which the characters are judged but a world view which underlies the system itself. For while objectively told, the events in *Crime and Punishment* do not take place only in the objective world. In the next to last sentence of the novel's final passage, the narrator speaks of Raskolnikov's encounter with a mode of being unknown to the dialectics of the self-contained rational intellect: "But that is the beginning

pp. 411–13; F. I. Evnin, "O nekotoryx voprosax stilja i poètiki Dostoevskogo," *Izvestija Akademii nauk*, 24, No. 1 (1965), 75–9; V. I. Ètov, "Manera povestvovanija v romane Dostoevskogo 'Idiot,'" *Vestnik Moskovskogo universiteta*, 21, No. 1 (1966), 70–5.

of a new story, of the gradual renewal of a man, of his gradual rebirth, his gradual transition from one world into another, his acquaintance with a new hitherto absolutely undreamed-of reality. This could constitute the theme of a new story — but our present one has come to an end." (423)

This new world and undreamed-of reality do not exist only in Raskolnikov's future, they are at the foundation of all the events in the novel. It is a higher reality which is at once transcendent and immanent, and which reveals itself in full force only in the epilogue. It is not, however, a plane of existence that we frequently encounter in the nineteenth-century novel, and this perhaps explains why so many critics have found fault with the characterization of Sonya, rejected the epilogue as artistically unjustified, and ignored the importance in the work of metaphysical reality. They have assumed that *Crime and Punishment*, like other nineteenth-century novels, has its foundation in the world of phenomena.

In most criticism of narrative genres, the novel is defined not only in formal terms of characterization, plot, symbolism, and the like, but by the nature of its fictional universe. It is generally regarded to be a prose narrative presenting characters in their social roles — as Fielding said, a comic epic in prose. And as such it is usually seen, in contrast to the romance, to have a strong foundation in objective material reality. Romance in this regard has a much greater latitude than the novel. Northrop Frye, in his *Anatomy of Criticism*, has eloquently expressed the different approach toward characterization between the genres in the following way:

> The romancer does not attempt to create "real people" so much as stylized figures which expand into psychological archetypes. ... That is why the romance so often radiates a glow of subjective intensity that the novel lacks, and why a suggestion of allegory is constantly creeping in around its fringes. Certain elements of character are released in the romance which make it naturally a more revolutionary form than the novel.[10]

It would be, to be sure, an exaggeration, if not an inaccuracy, to call *Crime and Punishment* a romance and not a novel; yet the world of *Crime and Punishment* has many affinities with that of romance, in which the laws of objective reality are often superseded. Although the

---

[10] *Anatomy of Criticism: Four Essays* (Princeton: Princeton Univ. Press, 1957), pp. 304–5.

contemporary social world plays an important role in *Crime and Punishment*, it is ultimately less crucial to the novel than the metaphysical order underpinning it.[11] This is certainly not the case with most nineteenth-century novels, in which the characters' lives are totally encompassed by objective material reality. Jane Austen and Emile Zola, no matter how great their differences, share common philosophical presuppositions about the world that set them off from such idealist writers as Hoffmann, Gogol, and Dostoevsky.

It is the function of the personalized narrator to persuade the reader to accept, at least artistically, the validity of the fictional universe in *Crime and Punishment*. If the novel is to hang together as an organic whole, the reader must be convinced that the religious reality which manifests itself so forcefully in the epilogue is not a gratuitous superimposition, but an objectively existing force which not only influences the characters but offers them concrete and meaningful choices. The personalized narrator guarantees that this is so. A totally objective narrator, on the other hand, would most certainly have left us with the strong possibility that Sonya's God was, as Raskolnikov implies, simply a symptom of her religious mania.

The religious substructure of the novel is not merely implied, it is supported by numerous details throughout. Even Western critics, however, have tended to ignore the evidence. Little attention has been devoted, for example, to the latent causes of Raskolnikov's regeneration; yet it is perhaps somewhat unjustified on our part to assume that Dostoevsky would have totally neglected to anchor the resurrection in Raskolnikov's personality; that he would have placed the whole burden of proof on the inscrutable nature of the religious miracle — to be sure, a philosophically sound way out, but hardly a credible and satisfying one aesthetically.[12] We know, for example, from his mother's letter that Raskolnikov had a strict religious upbringing, that he lisped his prayers at his mother's knee, and that he believed in the mercy of "Our Creator and Redeemer". At that time he was unquestionably happy. In his first

---

[11] Dostoevsky was always acutely aware that at bottom his realism was much closer to idealism than to the realism of his contemporaries. Like all idealists, he argued that his idealism was more real than the realism of the so-called realists. For his numerous statements on realism with regard to his own work and the works of others, see Sven Linnér, *Dostoevskij on Realism* (Stockholm: Almquist and Wiksell, 1967).

[12] For a discussion of the artistic representation of the miracle in Dostoevsky, see L. A. Zander, *Dostoevsky*, trans. by Natalie Duddington (London: SCM Press, 1948), pp. 15–25.

dream he remembers that as a child, whenever he visited the grave of his little brother, he used to religiously and reverently cross himself and bow down and kiss the little grave. He remembers how he loved the church to which he would be taken two to three times a year to observe a service held in memory of his grandmother.

Nor is it strange that he should stop on his way home from the university precisely at that spot where the cupola of St. Isaac's Cathedral shone in its most dazzling splendor. Transfixed, he would gaze "at this truly magnificent spectacle and almost always would marvel at a vague and mysterious emotion it roused in him". (91) Although this spectacle leaves him cold when he passes it after the murder, we are conscious that Raskolnikov holds deep within him the seeds of a new reality, which in the past were stirred by this beautiful sight, and which will flower when he has sufficiently atoned for his transgression.[13]

Especially significant with regard to Raskolnikov's beliefs is the scene in which he explains his article on crime to Porfiry. He mentions the New Jerusalem, whereupon Porfiry asks him if he believes in it. Raskolnikov says he does. Porfiry presses on:

"A–and do you believe in God? Excuse my curiosity."
"I do," repeated Raskolnikov, raising his eyes to Porfiry.
"A–and do you believe in Lazarus' rising from the dead?"
"I–I do. Why do you ask all this?"
"You believe it literally?"
"Literally."
"You don't say so. ... I asked from curiosity. Excuse me. ..." (203–4)

Soviet critics have naturally interpreted the New Jerusalem in this passage as an allusion to the socialist utopia of Saint-Simon.[14] But this interpretation does not satisfactorily explain Raskolnikov's other answers to the questions put to him; for he tells Porfiry that he not only believes in God, but also in Lazarus' resurrection from the dead. Porfiry obviously shares the same doubts as the reader; consequently Dostoevsky has him ask Raskolnikov if he believes in Lazarus' resurrection literally. Raskolnikov

---

[13] There are, of course, other important facts pointing to Raskolnikov's latent religious side. After the dream of the beaten horse, Raskolnikov prays to God to show him the way by which he may renonunce his "accursed dream". (51) He asks Polechka to pray for him when she invites him to her step-father's (Marmeladov's) funeral feast. (148) Toward the end of the novel, in deep earnest, he also asks his mother to pray for him. (398–9)

[14] See, for example, V. Ja. Kirpotin, *Razočarovanie i krušenie Rodiona Raskol'nikova* (M.: Sov. pisatel', 1972), p. 111; G. F. Kogan, *CP*, p. 756.

answers in the affirmative. Moreover, the scene at which Sonya reads Raskolnikov the passage about Lazarus' rising from the dead shows that at least some part of him is speaking the truth when he says he believes it literally. Raskolnikov's request that Sonya read him this passage constitutes psychological evidence of his yearning, however suppressed, to believe in the possibility of salvation.

But the Lazarus scene does more than merely offer proof of Raskolnikov's latent religiousness; it reveals the underlying religious vision of the novel through the narrator:

"This is all about the raising of Lazarus," she whispered sternly and abruptly, and turning away she stood motionless, not daring, almost ashamed, to raise her eyes to him. Her feverish trembling continued. The candle had long since reached its end in the twisted candlestick, dimly illuminating in the poverty-stricken room the murderer and the harlot, who had so strangely come together to read the Eternal Book. Five minutes or more passed. (254)

As was shown in Chapter Six, this passage clearly indicates that the narrator believes in the validity of the Bible and consequently the implications it has for both hero and heroine. The language is solemn; there is no irony. Since he has proven to be absolutely reliable elsewhere in the novel, the reader is compelled to accept the Biblical truths as valid not only for the Lazarus scene, but for the entire novel. We suspend our disbelief; for the narrator's point of view is not, as Bakhtin maintains, just another opinion, but a higher point of view, which the reader has grown to accept and trust.

The narrator's statements in the epilogue regarding Raskolnikov's experience of a hitherto-unknown reality further establish the novel's metaphysical world view. His exultant report of Raskolnikov's transformation and less critical view of Sonya's beliefs assure the reader that the religious reality, however subtly portrayed in the novel proper, is nonetheless in full force; that it is the fundamental reality. The omniscient narrator personally vouches for the authenticity of the events. Thus not only does he unify *Crime and Punishment* by subordinating all points of view to his own, he also validates the fictional universe from which these points of view derive their ultimate relevance.

BIBLIOGRAPHY OF EDITIONS

Dostoevskij, F. M., *Iz arxiva F. M. Dostoevskogo, "Prestuplenie i nakazanie,"* ed. I. I. Glivenko (M., L., 1931).
—, *Pis'ma*, ed. A. S. Dolinin, 4 vols. (M., L., 1928–59).
—, *Polnoe sobranie sočinenij*, ed. V. G. Bazanov et al., 30 vols. [projected] (L., 1972–).
—, *Polnoe sobranie xudožestvennyx proizvedenij*, ed. V. B. Tomaševskij and K. I. Xalabaev, 13 vols. (M., L., 1926–30).
—, *Prestuplenie i nakazanie*, ed. L. D. Opul'skaja and G. F. Kogan (M., 1970).
—, *Sobranie sočinenij*, ed. L. P. Grossman et al., 10 vols. (M.: 1956–8).
Flaubert, Gustave, "Madame Bovary," *Oeuvres complètes*, I (1971).
—, *Madame Bovary*, trans. Paul de Man (New York, 1965).
Joyce, James, *Portrait of the Artist as a Young Man* (New York, 1964).

SELECTED BIBLIOGRAPHY OF
SCHOLARLY WORKS

Auerbach, Eric, *Mimesis: The Representation of Reality in Western Literature*, trans. Willard Trask (Princeton, 1953).

Baxtin, M. M., *Problemy poètiki Dostoevskogo*, 2nd ed. (M., 1963).

Beach, Joseph Warren, *The Twentieth Century Novel: Studies in Technique* (New York, 1932).

Beebe, Maurice, "The Three Motives of Raskolnikov: A Reinterpretation of 'Crime and Punishment,' " *College English*, 17 (1955), 151–8.

Belkin, A. A., *Čitaja Dostoevskogo i Čexova: Stat'i i razbory* (M., 1973).

Blackmur, R. P., " 'Crime and Punishment': A Study of Dostoevsky," in *Essays in Modern Literary Criticism*, ed. Ray B. West (New York, 1952), pp. 472–489.

Bogdanov, V. A., "Proverim tipologiju: Sjužet i kompozicija sjužeta v romane 'Prestuplenie i nakazanie,' " *Filologičeskie nauki*, 13, No. 6 (1970), 74–80.

Bojko, M. N., "Vnutrennij monolog v proizvedenijax L. N. Tolstogo i F. M. Dostoevskogo," in *L. N. Tolstoj: Sbornik statej o tvorčestve*, ed. N. K. Gudzij (M., 1959), pp. 83–99.

Bonwit, Marianne, "Gustave Flaubert et le principe d'impassibilité," *University of California Publications in Modern Philology*, 33, No. 4 (1950), 263–420.

Booth, Wayne, "Distance and Point of View: An Essay in Classification," *Essays in Criticism*, 11 (1961), 60–79.

—, *The Rhetoric of Fiction* (Chicago, 1961).

Bowling, Lawrence E., "What is the Stream of Consciousness Technique?" *PMLA*, 65 (1950), 333–45.

Cejtlin, A. G., *Masterstvo Puškina* (M., 1938).

Černyševskij, N. G., *Literaturno-kritičeskie stat'i*, ed. N. F. Belčikov (M., 1939).

Čičerin, A. B. "Poètičeskij stroj jazyka v romanax Dostoevskogo," in *Tvorčestvo F. M. Dostoevskogo*, ed. N. L. Stepanov (M., 1959), pp. 417–44.

Čirkov, N. M., *O stile Dostoevskogo* (M., 1967).

Cohn, Dorrit, "Narrated Monologue: Definition of a Fictional Style," *Comparative Literature*, 18 (1966), 97–112.

Čulkov, G. I., *Kak rabotal Dostoevskij* (M., 1939).

Curle, Richard, *Characters of Dostoevsky: Studies from Four Novels* (London, 1950).

Dauner, Louise, "Raskolnikov in Search of a Soul," *Modern Fiction Studies*, 4 (1958), 199–210.

Davidovič, M. G., "Problema zanimatel'nosti v romanax Dostoevskogo," in *Tvorčeskij put' Dostoevskogo*, ed. N. L. Brodskij (L., 1924), pp. 104–31.

Dujardin, Edouard, *Le monologue intérieur* (Paris, 1930).

Eastman, Richard M., "Idea and Method in a Scene by Dostoevsky," *College English*, 17 (1955), 143–50.

Ètov, V. I., *Dostoevskij: Očerk tvorčestva* (M., 1968).
—, "Manera povestvovanija v romane Dostoevskogo 'Idiot,'" *Vestnik Moskovskogo universiteta*, 21, No. 1 (1966), 70–6.
—, "Priemy psixologičeskogo analiza v romane 'Prestuplenie i nakazanie,'" *Vestnik Moskovskogo Universiteta*, 22, No. 3 (1967), 3–13.
Evnin, F. I. "O nekotoryx voprosax stilja i poètiki Dostoevskogo," *Izvestija Akademii Nauk*, 24, No. 1 (1965), 68–80.
—, "Roman 'Prestuplenie i nakazanie,'" in *Tvorčestvo Dostoevskogo*, ed. N. L. Stepanov (M., 1959), pp. 128–72.
Fanger, Donald, *Dostoevsky and Romantic Realism* (Chicago, 1965).
Fehr, Bernhard, "Substitutionary Narration and Description," *English Studies*, 20 (1938), 97–107.
Forster, E. M., *Aspects of the Novel* (New York, 1927).
Frank, Joseph, "The World of Raskolnikov," *Encounter*, 26 (June, 1966), 30–5.
Fridlender, G. M., *Realizm Dostoevskogo* (M., L., 1964).
Friedemann, Käte, *Die Rolle des Erzählers in der Epik* (Leipzig, 1910).
Friedman, Melvin, *Stream of Consciousness: A Study in Literary Method* (New Haven, 1955).
Friedman, Norman, "Point of View in Fiction: The Development of a Critical Concept," *PMLA*, 70 (1955), 1160–84.
Frye, Northrop, *Anatomy of Criticism: Four Essays* (1957; rpt. New York, 1967).
Gerigk, Horst-Jürgen, *Versuch über Dostoevskijs "Jüngling": Ein Beitrag zur Theorie des Romans* (Munich, 1965).
Gibian, George, "Traditional Symbolism in 'Crime and Punishment,'" *PMLA*, 70 (1955), 979–96.
Gibson, A. Boyce, *The Religion of Dostoevsky* (London, 1973).
Grossman, L. P., "Dostoevskij — xudožnik," in *Tvorčestvo Dostoevskogo*, ed. N. L. Stepanov (M., 1959), pp. 330–416.
—, *Poètika Dostoevskogo* (M., 1925).
—, "Problema realizma u Dostoevskogo," *Vestnik Evropy*, (Feb., 1917), pp. 65–100.
Hackel, Sergei, "Raskolnikov Through the Looking-Glass: Dostoevsky and Camus's 'L'Etranger,'" *Wisconsin Studies in Contemporary Literature*, 9 (1968), 189–209.
Hamburger, Käte, *Die Logik der Dichtung*, 2nd ed. (Stuttgart, 1968).
Hanan, David, "'Crime and Punishment': The Idea of the Crime," *The Critical Review*, 12 (1969), 15–28.
Hart, Pierre E., "Looking Over Raskol'nikov's Shoulder: The Narrator in 'Crime and Punishment,'" *Criticism*, 13 (1971), 166–79.
Harvey, W. J., "George Eliot and the Omniscient Author Convention," *Nineteenth-Century Fiction*, 13 (Sept. 1958), 81–108.
Holthusen, Johannes, *Prinzipien der Komposition und des Erzählens bei Dostoevskij* (Köln, 1969).
Humphrey, Robert, *Stream of Consciousness in the Modern Novel* (Berkeley, 1954).
Ingarden, Roman, *Issledovanija po èstetike*, trans. A. Ermilov and B. Fedorov (M., 1962).
Ivanov, Vyacheslav, *Freedom and the Tragic Life: A Study in Dostoevsky*, trans. Norman Cameron (London, 1952).
James, Henry, *The Art of the Novel: Critical Prefaces*, introd. R. P. Blackmur (New York, 1934).
Karanči, László, "K problematike pisatel'skoj manery Dostoevskogo," *Slavica*, 1 (1961), 135–55.

Kayser, Wolfgang, *Entstehung und Krise des modernen Romans*, 2nd ed. (Stuttgart, 1955).

—, "Wer erzählt den Roman?" in *Die Vortragsreise* (Berne, 1958), pp. 83–101.

Kirpotin, V. Ja., *Razočarovanie i krušenie Rodiona Raskol'nikova: Kniga o romane F. M. Dostoevskogo "Prestuplenie i nakazanie"* (M., 1970).

Komroff, Manuel, "View-point," in *Dictionary of World Literature*, ed. Joseph T. Shipley (Totowa, New Jersey, 1968).

Kovtunova, I. I. "Nesobstvenno-prjamaja reč' v sovremennom russkom literaturnom jazyke," *Russkij jazyk v škole*, 14, No. 2 (1953), 18–27.

Krag, Erik, "Neskol'ko zamečanij po povodu stilja Dostoevskogo," *Scando-Slavica*, 9 (1963), 22–36.

Lämmert, Eberhard, *Bauformen des Erzählens*, 2nd ed. (Stuttgart, 1967).

Leatherbarrow, W. J., "Raskolnikov and the 'Enigma of his Personality,'" *Forum for Modern Language Studies*, 9 (1973), 153–65.

Lethcoe, Ronald James, "Narrated Speech and Narrated Consciousness," Diss. Univ. of Wisconsin, 1969.

Linnér, Sven *Dostoevskij on Realism* (Stockholm, 1967).

Lixačev, Dmitrij, "Letopisnoe vremja' u Dostoevskogo," in *Poètika drevnerusskoj literatury* (L., 1967), pp. 319–34.

Lockhart, Adrienne, "Life and Dialectics: A Further Reading of 'Crime and Punishment,'" *Balcony*, No. 3 (1965), pp. 51–5.

Lubbock, Percy, *The Craft of Fiction* (1921; rpt. New York, 1957).

Lukács, Georg, *Die Theorie des Romans* (Berlin, 1920).

Lunačarskij, A. V., "O 'mnogogolosnosti' Dostoevskogo," in *F. M. Dostoevskij v russkoj kritike: Sbornik statej*, ed. A. A. Belkin (M., 1956), pp. 403–29.

Lutwack, Leonard, "Mixed and Uniform Prose Styles in the Novel," *Journal of Aesthetics and Art Criticism*, 18 (1960), 350–7.

Mackiewicz, Stanislaw, *Dostoevsky* (London, 1947).

Marx, Paul, "A Defense of the Epilogue to 'Crime and Punishment,'" *Bucknell Review*, 10 (1961), 57–74.

Matlaw, Ralph E., "Recurrent Imagery in Dostoevsky," *Harvard Slavic Studies*, 3 (Cambridge, Mass., 1957), pp. 201–25.

Maurina, Zenta, *A Prophet of the Soul: Fyodor Dostoievsky*, trans. C. P. Finlayson (London, 1940).

McDonald, Walter R., "Dostoevsky's 'Crime and Punishment,'" *Explicator*, 26 (1968).

Meier-Graefe, Julius, *Dostoevsky: The Man and His Work*, trans. Herbert H. Marks (New York, 1928).

Meijer, J. M., "Situation Rhyme in a Novel of Dostoevskij," *Dutch Contributions to the Fourth International Congress of Slavicists* (The Hague, 1958), pp. 115–28.

Mejer, Georgij, "Svet i noči: Opyt medlennogo čtenija," *Grani*, No. 51 (1962), pp. 120–39.

Merežkovskij, D. S., *L. Tolstoj i Dostoevskij: Žizn', tvorčestvo, i religija* in *Polnoe sobranie sočinenij*, 7 (St. P., 1912).

Mirsky, D. S., *A History of Russian Literature from the Earliest Times to the Death of Dostoevsky* (New York, 1927).

Mochulsky, Konstantin, *Dostoevsky: His Life and Work*, trans. Michael A. Minihan (Princeton, 1967).

Mortimer, Ruth, "Dostoevski and the Dream," *Modern Philology*, 54 (Nov. 1956), 106–16.

Murry, John Middleton, *Fyodor Dostoevsky: A Critical Study* (London, 1923).

Mysljakov, V. A., "Kak rasskazana 'istorija' Rodiona Raskol'nikova," in *Dostoevskij: Materialy i issledovanija*, ed. G. M. Fridlender (L., 1974), pp. 147–63.

Niemi, Pearl C., "The Art of 'Crime and Punishment,'" *Modern Fiction Studies*, 9 (1964), 291–313.

Ohmann, Richard M., "Prolegomena to the Analysis of Prose Style," *Style in Prose Fiction: English Institute Essays*, ed. Harold Martin (New York, 1959).

Opul'skaja, L. D., "Istorija sozdanija romana," in *F. M. Dostoevskij, "Prestuplenie i nakazanie*," ed. L. D. Opul'skaja and F. G. Kogan (M., 1970), pp. 681–715.

Peace, Richard, *Dostoevsky: An Examination of the Major Novels* (Cambridge, 1971).

Pereverzev, V. F., *Tvorčestvo Dostoevskogo* (M., 1928).

Rahv, Philip, "Dostoevsky in 'Crime and Punishment,'" *Partisan Review*, 27 (1960), 393–425.

Reeve, F. D., "In the Stinking City: Dostoevskij's 'Crime and Punishment,'" *Slavic and East European Journal*, 14 (1960), 127–36.

Riemer, A. P., "The Charted City: A Reading of 'Crime and Punishment,'" *Balcony*, No. 1 (1965), pp. 15–22.

Robbe-Grillet, Alain, *For a New Novel: Essays on Fiction*, trans. Richard Howard (New York, 1965).

Roe, Ivan, *The Breath of Corruption: An Interpretation of Dostoievsky* (London, 1946).

Romberg, Bertil, *Studies in the Narrative Technique of the First-person Novel* (Stockholm, 1962).

Rubin, Louis, D. Jr., *The Teller in the Tale* (Seattle, 1967).

Sarraute, Nathalie, "The Age of Suspicion," in *The Age of Suspicion*, trans. Maria Julas (New York, 1963), pp. 51–74.

Schmid, Wolf, *Der Textaufbau in den Erzählungen Dostoevskijs* (Munich, 1973).

Scholes, Robert and Robert Kellogg, *The Nature of Narrative* (New York, 1966).

Shaw, J. Thomas, "The 'Conclusion' of Pushkin's *Queen of Spades*," in *Studies in Russian and Polish Literatures in Honor of Waclaw Lednicki* (The Hague, 1962), pp. 114–26.

—, "Raskol'nikov's Dreams," *Slavic and East European Journal*, 17 (1973), 131–145.

Simmons, Ernest J., *Dostoevsky: The Making of a Novelist* (1940; rpt. London, 1950).

Šklovskij, V. B., *O teorii prozy* (M., 1929).

—, *Povesti o proze: Razmyšlenija i razbory*, II (M., 1966).

—, *Za i protiv: Zametki o Dostoevskom* (M., 1957).

Slonimskij, A. L., "'Vdrug' u Dostoevskogo," *Kniga i revoljucija*, No. 8 (1922), pp. 9–16.

Snodgrass, W. D., "'Crime and Punishment': The Tenor of Part One," *Hudson Review*, 13 (1960), 202–53.

Sokolova, L. A., *Nesobstvenno-avtorskaja (nesobstvenno-prjamaja) reč' kak stilističeskaja kategorija* (Tomsk, 1968).

Stanzel, Franz, "Episches Praeteritum, erlebte Rede, historisches Praesens," *Deutsche Vierteljahrsschrift für Literaturwissenschaft und Geistesgeschichte*, 33 (1959), 1–12.

—, *Typische Formen des Romans*, 2nd ed. (Göttingen, 1965).

Steinmann, Martin, Jr., "The Old Novel and the New," in *From Jane Austen to Joseph Conrad*, ed. Robert C. Rathburn and Martin Steinmann, Jr. (Minneapolis, 1958), pp. 286–306.

Struve, Gleb, "'Monologue intérieur': The Origins of the Formula and the First Statement of its Possibilities," *PMLA*, 69 (1954), 1101–11.

Thibaudet, Albert, *Réflexions sur le roman*, 6th ed. (Paris, 1938).

Tilford, John E., Jr., "James the Old Intruder," *Modern Fiction Studies*, 4 (Summer, 1958), 157–64.

Tillotson, Kathleen, *The Tale and the Teller* (London, 1959).

Tomaševskij, B. V., *Teorija literatury: Poètika*, 3rd ed. (M., 1927).

Toporov, V. N., "O strukture romana Dostoevskogo 'Prestuplenie i nakazanie,'" in *Structure of Texts and Semiotics of Culture*, ed. Jan van der Eng and Mojmír Grygar (The Hague, 1973), pp. 225–302.

Trubetzkoy, N. S., *Dostoevskij als Künstler* (The Hague, 1964).

van der Eng, Johannes, *Dostoevskij romancier: Rapports entre sa vision du monde et ses procédés littéraires* (The Hague, 1957).

Vinogradov, I. and N. Denisova, "Sovsem tut drugie pričiny...(Ljus'en de Rjubempre i Rodion Raskol'nikov: Opyt sravnitel'nogo analiza)," *Voprosy literatury*, 16, No. 10 (1972), 76–106.

Walzel, Oskar, *Das Wortkunstwerk: Mittel seiner Erforschung* (Leipzig, 1926).

Wasiolek, Edward, *Dostoevsky: The Major Fiction* (Cambridge: M.I.T. Press, 1964).

—, ed. and trans., *Fyodor Dostoevsky, The Notebooks for "Crime and Punishment"* (Chicago, 1967).

—, "On the Structure of 'Crime and Punishment,'" *PMLA*, 74 (1959), 131–6.

Wellek, René and Austin Warren, *Theory of Literature*, 3rd ed. (New York, 1956).

Willett, Maurita, "The 'Ending' of *Crime and Punishment*," *Orbis Litterarum*, 25 (1970), 244–58.

Woolf, Virginia, *Mr. Bennet and Mrs. Brown* (London, 1924).

Yarmolinsky, Avrahm, *Dostoevsky: His Life and Art* (New York, 1957).

Zander, L. A., *Dostoevsky*, trans. Natalie Duddington (London, 1948).

Zundelovič, Ja. O., *Romany Dostoevskogo: Stat'i* (Taškent, 1963).